AMERICAN RUINS

AMERICAN RUINS

CAMILO JOSÉ VERGARA

THE MONACELLI PRESS

Contents

First published in the United States of America in 1999 by
The Monacelli Press, Inc.
10 East 92nd Street, New York, New York 10128.

Library of Congress Cataloging-in-Publication Data
Vergara, Camilo J.
American ruins / Camilo José Vergara.
p. cm.
Includes bibliographical references.
ISBN 1-58093-056-5
1. Inner cities—United States. 2. Inner cities—United States—
Pictorial works. I. Title
HN59.2.V47 1999
307.76'0973—dc21   99-35505

Printed and bound in Italy

Designed by Ink, Inc.

FRONT COVER: *Blackstone
Building, Gary, 1996. The grimy,
smoke-darkened building stood
for more than half a century
near the Gary Works, one of the
largest steel-producing facilities
in the United States. The steel
plant, modernized and run
mainly by machines, thrives,
but the Blackstone Building was
razed in 1998.*

BACK COVER: *Packard
Automobile Plant (now Motor
City Industrial Park), Detroit,
1998. Parts of the three-and-a-
half-million-square-foot plant
(which stopped producing
automobiles in 1956) are used for
raves and paint-pellet war games.*

FRONTISPIECE: *Detail of a
mansion, downtown Los Angeles,
1996. The columns recall
Baudelaire's memorable phrase
"great columns, upright and
majestic."*

OPPOSITE: *Ruined farmers'
market, Gary, 1995. Only the
impressive steel armature
remains.*

Energies of the Outmoded

These are the ruins of a civilization that astonished the world.
—Robert Fishman, historian, 1998

Urban ruination is serious; it is real; it is not a stage set; it has spiritual authenticity. Symbols of modern life have turned into symbols of death. There is nothing like it in the suburbs. Getting down to the bottom of things puts you in touch with some kind of ultimate reality.
—Marshall Berman, 1999

Who speaks of winning—to survive is everything.
—Rainer Maria Rilke

1

I *Children playing basketball among the ruins of a gas station, Gary, 1997. Upon seeing me with a camera, they ran into their houses to put their new Chicago Bulls T-shirts on. A year later, during another visit, I saw them again and showed them a barely legible copy of this photo. "That's me, I had two pony tails," exclaimed one girl. Others chimed in: "That is Willie and that is Dwayne"; "My brother is over there"; "I remember when you took this picture; I had my panties rolled." They gave me their addresses and asked me to send them copies.*

URBANITY IN DECAY

American Ruins documents and interprets the demise, reuse, and replacement of the buildings and structures that once defined the industrial city: skyscrapers, factories, hospitals, theaters, apartment buildings, churches, warehouses, courthouses, police stations, mansions, entire city blocks, and, in the case of Detroit, the whole pre-Depression skyline. I have photographed the exteriors of ruined buildings and, whenever possible, their interiors at some seventy sites in New York City; Newark; Detroit; Camden, New Jersey; Philadelphia; Baltimore; Chicago; Gary, Indiana; and Los Angeles. I have interviewed residents and officials and delved into the historical archives.

The project grew naturally out of *The New American Ghetto* (1995), my documentation of the evolution of the built environment in the country's largest and most devastated ghettos. I turned my attention to the widespread ruination of industrial cities of the East and the Midwest, particularly Detroit and Chicago, in order to interpret the meaning of ruins in the life of cities. In contrast to those who see these ruins as failures and eyesores that are best forgotten, I record urban decay with a combined sense of respect, loss, and admiration for its peculiar beauty.

The legacies of four distinct building traditions dominate this book. First is that of the Beaux-Arts palace, popularized by the Chicago World's Fair of 1893 and the "Gallic-inspired designs for monuments, museums and other excellent things." This grand style for public building is represented in this book by the former Bronx Borough Courthouse, the Gary train station, and the Camden Free Public Library. The American character of these buildings rests on the belief, at the time of their construction, that the new democratic culture would embody the best ideas the Old World had to offer. Second is the tradition of industrial structures of reinforced concrete, among them the pioneering Packard Automobile Plant in Detroit and the RCA Victor complex in Camden. With their simple forms, enormous scale, and impressive new technologies, these structures were the very definition of modernity in the first half of this century.

Post–World War II structures form the third tradition, represented by high-rise housing projects, streamlined gas stations, and cheap cinderblock structures; in this book are the Henry Horner Homes (2051 West Lake) in Chicago and an old tire dealership in Detroit, among others. A fourth tradition is that of vernacular structures: homes, stores, and small factories that despite their light construction survived for as

2 *Across from Cabrini Green in Chicago, a 1998 version of Jacob Riis's 1887 photograph of New York City's Lower East Side,* Bandit's Roost.

long as their owners were willing to maintain them. (See, for example, the collapsed two-story frame house in Detroit that introduces chapter 2.) These structures make up the bulk of the built environment and are usually the first to be demolished.

The term "American ruins" might seem to contradict itself, for the United States is a nation conventionally synonymous with innovation and resilience, modernity and progress. In the 1920s and 1930s European visitors like Le Corbusier, Fritz Lang, Walter Gropius, and Erich Mendelsohn were amazed at the size and dynamism of urban America. Gropius claimed to be "overwhelmed by the city and the scale of buildings," and Mendelsohn described American cities as "unbridled, mad, frenetic, lusting for life." But today many of the structures that so impressed Europeans are in decay, and the communities that grew up around them are being discarded and destroyed at a pace that might also be described as unbridled, mad, and frenetic. While the United States remains a leader in industry and technology, it also now leads the world in the number, size, and degradation of its abandoned structures.

I happened to come to the United States during a period when people and capital were abandoning the cities, at time when the economy was relocating to the suburban periphery and domestic industries were expanding to locations all over the world. Along the emptying residential streets, on commercial and industrial blocks, I have wit-

3 *Pulaski Road, West Side of Chicago, 1998.*

nessed the ways in which residents, companies, and public officials have used, demolished, or sometimes even rebuilt what was left behind.

Many magnificent buildings have already disappeared or are being demolished. Factories lie rusting, their cavernous interiors dark, their roofs covered with greenery, demolition their sure fate. Schools and libraries are closed, and once vibrant neighborhoods have been reduced to empty lots and scattered houses. A number of substantial edifices in older industrial cities have survived only because of their size, the quality of their materials, and the sheer expense of demolishing such large, solid structures. City officials are sometimes reluctant to raze buildings that for decades may have been symbols of the city, particularly when replacement structures are likely to be parking lots or fast-food franchises.

Municipalities have developed several strategies to deal with ruins. Sealing structures prevents people from getting hurt, from scavenging, and from squatting. To improve the image of the city, officials put colorful decals over broken windows and doors, add awnings to vacant skyscrapers, and even paint new facades to make derelict buildings seem occupied. By creating contemporary Potemkin villages, officials hope to lure investors to their cities. Preservationists, who usually live outside the ghetto, rarely cross its borders to save endangered buildings in the less desirable parts of town. Black and Latino elected officials are reluctant to commit scarce resources to reclaim buildings that once welcomed people of color only as shoeshine boys, elevator operators, janitors, foundry workers, and maids.

Moving is a time-honored way to improve one's condition in the United States. People migrate to suburban neighborhoods for more space and greenery and to feel that they have greater control over their environments. Government policies at all levels continue to favor suburban growth and development, facilitating disinvestment in the urban core by providing the legal framework and financial support to enable the periphery to isolate itself from poverty and crime. Yet a new phase in urban development is evident. Taking advantage of excellent transportation systems that lead to their downtowns, many cities are building new sport facilities, casinos, aquariums, and hotels. The expressways that were once instrumental in emptying urban cores now help to bring visitors back to the center. Ironically, as municipalities discover a future—however precarious—in tourism, entertainment, and culture, destruction continues to menace some of the oldest and grandest structures. Delighted that something is finally being done about derelict downtowns, officials help developers by condemning buildings that are in the way. They even contribute public funds to buy the land out from under them and pay for demolition.

Contemporary industrial spaces, "the mines and foundries of the information age," as Manuel Castells calls them, are often located in campus-like settings at the periphery of large metropolitan areas. The production for these sites, whose function is to "generate the basic materials of the information economy," takes place hundreds of miles away, in low, anonymous, warehouse-like structures, stylistically disconnected from the past. Such structures have failed to capture the public imagination. In 1999 Mitchell Schwartzer described Silicon Valley office architecture as consisting mainly of rented structures that are "above all alterable and exchangeable." He added that they are easy

for corporations to rent to successive tenants because they lack specific signifying decoration and are therefore undifferentiated from one another.

The image of the industrial city remains powerful. Much physical labor and resources went into the construction and operation of now decaying factories, where skilled workers once put together products that gave them a sense of pride and identity. The factory-made ensembles of pieces could be taken apart with a screwdriver; ordinary people could understand how they functioned; they were grounded in a specific site of production. Many of the industrial city's great buildings are still widely recognizable symbols, and its products are still prized for their quality and beautiful design. It is this aura of youth and optimism, colored by nostalgia, that represents the nation's memories of city life in countless movies and television programs.

A "SMITHSONIAN OF DECLINE"

My photographs, exhibitions, and articles on downtown Detroit helped begin a national dialogue on the future of urban ruins. Without pretending that structures in the process of being discarded can retain their former economic and social importance, I continue to argue that their power as symbols remains strong. They are an essential part of understanding America.

4 *An old streamlined Oklahoma Gas Station with porcelain enamel exterior, West Side of Detroit, 1998.*

5 *Ruined split-level house, part of a subsidized development, Ford Heights, Illinois, 1991.*

5

That urban ruins have acquired new meanings—that they are now being used by such marginal groups as homeless people, addicts, prostitutes, goth rockers, adventurous teenagers, and artists—is of no importance to an institution like the Smithsonian, whose function is to create a mainstream consensus. Its motto, inscribed on a 1946 postage stamp: "For the Increase and Diffusion of Knowledge Among Men."

The "nation's attic," an enormous institution, shows no concern for the current condition of the places that produced the objects it so proudly houses. What would Senator X say if a record of urban destruction were placed alongside these objects to haunt viewers? I imagine him saying, "None of this junk for the Mall; it makes my constituents feel bad. America is young. Stick to space exploration, to Silicon Valley, to Hollywood. If we want to refer to the past, we'll show Shaker furniture and quilts. Yes, keep a selection of the best examples of American machines and products, but keep them new and shining, as if fresh off the assembly line: an International Harvester fire truck, the original Mickey Mouse, a 1948 Packard, a stained-glass window depicting RCA Victor's listening dog, 'Nipper,' and a still-blinking neon sign."

My "Smithsonian of Decline" is much more interested in downtown Detroit. I would do nothing but secure the buildings and would allow the passage of time to create an urban ruins park, an American Acropolis. I want to display the derelict fire

truck, with its rusting lights and broken windows, that I saw in a poor suburb in the south of Chicago in the summer of 1998; the creepy effigy of Mickey I found in an alley in Gary in 1997; the shattered Nipper window of the former RCA plant that I photographed in Camden in 1997; and the dozens of extinguished neon signs ready to fall from their rusted supports. This book is a compendium of environments, structures, and things in the process of decline. In the mid-1970s, Bobby Wright, a black minister living in Newark's Central Ward, described his community as "robbed, burned up, yet still having a soul." *American Ruins* is a search among dereliction and destruction for that soul.

MY RUINS

My work consists of photographic documentation, exchanges with large numbers of diverse people, and long hours of reading and reflection. In the field, I approach passersby and shopkeepers to ask what the nearby abandoned and worn-out buildings mean to them. When taking a photograph I often wait for humans or animals to pass, giving a sense of scale and showing how they interact with the environment. I formulate questions based on what I see and ask those who walk by these places every day to comment. Many people feel comfortable speaking about their surroundings; some do not. The subject of a

6 *The remains of an old Montgomery Ward warehouse, West Side of Detroit, 1996.*

7 *Former parking lot of International Harvester, Components Division, West Pullman, Chicago, 1998. The tower of the Ingersoll Products plant looms in the background like a big eye on a stalk, surveying the parking lot.*

7

building or block is not as sensitive a topic as work, family life, or education, but I have occasionally encountered bafflement—and sometimes outright hostility:

> "It shall cost you $25 to take pictures there.
> Get him! Get him!"
> —*Homeless man, South Central Los Angeles, 1998*

> Mechanic: "Do you have an I.D. or something?"
> Me: "I am a freelance photographer."
> Mechanic: "Boss doesn't like that kind of shit."
> —*Tire Shop, Seven Mile Road, Detroit, 1998*

> "Do you know about the Indian? Do you know about the horse? Do you know about the Virgin? You want to speak about everything and you know nothing!"
> —*Erika, Botanica, Pico-Union, Los Angeles, 1998*

> "You are not a cop? An undercover cop?"
> —*Gerardo, gang member, South Central Los Angeles, 1996*

> "You are pirating our business!"
> —*Security guard, Casamientos Legales, Downtown Los Angeles, 1996*

"Get out of here! Get the fuck out of here!"
 —*Woman driver in Compton, Los Angeles, trying to run me over, 1996*

"I thought you were with the city or something."
 —*Shantelle's Beauty Salon, West Side of Chicago, 1996*

"Just shoot that guy."
 —*Black youth pointing at me, Brownsville, Brooklyn, 1997*

"Are you trying to bring black and white people together?"
 —*Lillie Roberts at the scene of a murder-suicide, Brownsville, Brooklyn, 1997*

To avoid unpleasant surprises, I look for signs of hostile people and dogs, and remain ever alert to physical dangers, lest I fall through a hole in the floor, trip on a broken step, or become trapped—all while deciding how best to capture the setting on film. I compare new pictures to earlier photos and assemble the old and new images into narrative groups. To elaborate upon these illustrated stories, I present them for discussion to both local residents and my friends outside the ghetto. Some of the most valuable contributions have come from repeated interviews with friends who were familiar with my work, had read the manuscript in draft, and were willing to help me as unofficial advisers on an ongoing basis.

8 *ABLA townhouses, Chicago, 1998. The gutted blocks of apartments are waiting for reconfiguration. The blocks will get pitched roofs at each end and new fenestration. Access to individual blocks of houses will be semiprivate.*

9 *Columbus Homes, Newark, 1994. Built in 1955, the housing was demolished in 1994. In the distance is the Cathedral of the Sacred Heart.*

9

I photograph objects, particularly those used in a close and intimate manner. Because these objects are pervasive parts of the world I document, I find it difficult to separate them from people. For the poet Heinrich Heine, such things live because people have given them a portion of their souls. Persistent objects—shopping carts, liquor bottles, cans of food, pieces of clothing, stuffed animals, improvised beds, and fading signs—follow people throughout their existence and reflect their lives.

My avocation reminds me of a particular extract from Fernando Pessoa's play *The Mariner* (1913):

> I dreamed of a mariner who appeared to be lost on a distant island. There were tall palm trees on the island, just a few, and faint birds passed over their motionless trunks . . . I couldn't see if they ever alighted . . . The mariner lived there, after surviving a shipwreck . . . As he had no means of returning to his homeland, and every time he remembered it he languished. He set himself to dream of a homeland that he'd never had; he set himself to create another homeland, another kind of land, with other kinds of landscapes, and another people, and another way of walking along the streets and leaning out of the windows . . . Every hour he constructed in his dream this false homeland, and he never left off dreaming . . .

In the beginning, he created the landscapes, then he created the cities; then the streets and the alleyways, one after another, carving them out of the stuff of his soul—street after street, district after district, right up to the walls of the quays where he then created the ports . . . Street after street, and the people who passed through them, and those who looked out on them from their windows . . . He began to recognize certain people, as if he was someone who scarcely knew them . . . Then he'd travel, after he'd memorized it, through the land he'd created . . . And in this way he gradually constructed his past . . . Soon he had another previous life . . . In that new homeland he now had a birthplace, the places where he'd passed his youth, ports where he'd embarked . . . He went on to have childhood companions, and then the friends and enemies of his manhood . . .

One day, when it had been raining heavily and the horizon was more indistinct, the mariner got tired of dreaming . . . He wanted to remember his one true homeland . . . but he realized that he couldn't remember any of it, that it no longer existed for him . . . The childhood he remembered was from the homeland of his dream, the adolescence that he recalled was the one he'd created . . . The whole of his life had been the life he had dreamed . . . And he saw that the other life could not possibly have existed . . . If he couldn't even remember a single street, person, or motherly gesture . . . And it was in the life he appeared to have dreamed that everything was real and had existed.

RETURNING TO RENGO

I am frequently asked what has made me devote decades to exploring ruined neighborhoods. The answer is that in the decaying cities of the United States I have found affinities with the Chilean town where I was raised. A visit to a ghetto makes me forget my problems. In the midst of decay and ruins I become completely engaged, contemplating structures both formerly magnificent and formerly humble, now undone.

I returned to my childhood home in 1990 to find not even a trace of it. My documentary methods aim at objectivity. But might I not be making this work an extension of my own personal history? To some extent, yes.

I grew up in the 1950s on a farm in Rengo, an agricultural town in Chile's central valley. At that time, Rengo had a population of eight thousand. Its movie theater offered a free annual showing of *Captain Blood*, starring Errol Flynn; its church was an old, dark adobe structure that smelled strongly of incense and bore on its walls the Stations of the Cross; its local cemetery was covered with rotting flowers. Wandering the streets were two insane but harmless men known to everybody by their nicknames, "Popeta" and "Cururo."

In the vast "nature preserves" of ghettos, I have experienced familiar sensations. Walking through vacant lots in the South Bronx in the early 1970s brought back to me the harsh smell of weeds and the pungent stench of rotten carcasses. Something primordial was restored to my life. I was surprised to experience as reassuring the sight and foul smell of a decomposed German shepherd covered with maggots.

In Rengo, buzzards always circled overhead. I lived near the town's slaughterhouse, where cattle, pigs, and lambs were butchered in much the same manner as they had been

10

10 *A 1948 International Harvester fire truck with its rusted searchlight pointed at the sky, East Chicago Heights (now Ford Heights), 1998. "The engine is perfect," said Captain McMath of the Ford Heights Fire Department. "If someone restored it, they would really have a truck."*

in the Middle Ages. Animals were taken from their pens and chained to the cement floor. Cows and sheep were killed with long knives. I remember hearing the scratching sounds of their hooves slipping on the wet cement and then the low thud of their bodies hitting the hard floor. Pigs were given blows on the head with a long, heavy hammer, and they wailed loudly and for a long time.

I was a hunter. I climbed hills and roamed through orchards, forests, and open fields searching for birds. My first weapon was a slingshot. My first kill, at age eight, was a rite of passage, even though it was a brown bird only a little bigger than a bumblebee. Later, a small rifle enabled me to kill enough birds to feed my family.

Digging holes was a favorite childhood pastime. The earth had a strong smell; in it I found broken combs, rusted nails, and tin cans. I was surprised at the variety of worms that lived underground: some were short, thick, and pearly white; others were long and brown. I believed that I could dig a tunnel that would take me to China. A friend later told me that I was pointed in the right direction.

Who could have predicted my later interest in urban decay? Rengo's backwardness soon embarrassed me. I loved the futurism of Flash Gordon comic books. I wanted to live in a modern city—with skyscrapers, elevated expressways, neon signs, and Art Deco buildings. To me the most beautiful object in the world was the brand-new 1956

11

Studebaker I saw parked in the town's main square. One of my most precious possessions was a small 1957 Zenith transistor radio. I remember how its round gold speaker shone against its burgundy plastic case. I even licked its cold exterior.

Declining family fortunes injected unpredictability and hopelessness into my surroundings. I came to despair of being able to change the course of my life. I felt that it was useless to plan when one could not count on even the most basic things. Early on I trained myself to be a witness, an onlooker—to be, as people put it, a useless person, an "Inspector Miranda," a busybody.

HOW I BECAME ACQUAINTED
WITH THE RUINS OF NORTH AMERICA

I was admitted to university, yet, drawn to the streets, neglected my studies. I could not pass the exams that would have allowed me to remain. In 1965, having exhausted my opportunities in Chile, I came to South Bend, Indiana, to study electrical engineering at the University of Notre Dame. I wanted to believe that science and technology would keep me from being poor, but my work habits did not change. I read Russian novels instead of studying. Soon after arriving in South Bend, I took a walk through the city's segregated west side. There I encountered my first American slums.

Then, in 1967, I read a passage in *Time Magazine*:

In traditionally red-lit, back-of-the-barroom pads along Gary's Washington Street—at Gus's Lounge, the Club Little Island, and the Central Cafe—the girls charge twenty to one hundred dollars and work in shifts to avoid occupational fatigue. Outside, Negro boys, few older than ten, lead the way to Adams and Jefferson Streets, just around the corner, where their sisters stand in the doorways, or sit by the windows—waving, winking, blowing kisses and tapping on the windows at potential Johns. At the sleazier local hotels, the guests all seem to be named Mr. and Mrs. Smith.

The article made nearby Gary, Indiana, irresistible to me. I convinced a friend to go along with me for a visit. With my eyes smarting from the smoke of the steel plants, I saw people gambling and drinking. I wanted to join them, but I felt alien and had little money; I could only look. My first trip to this foul-smelling city on a hot, humid summer day was one of the most memorable of my college years. Since that day in the 1960s, I have gone back to Gary perhaps a hundred times. Now the city is ruined, but the air is clean. The prostitutes seem old and dead-eyed. Still I remain intensely attracted to the leftovers of Steel City.

In urban America I found the challenge of my life. I became so attached to derelict buildings that sadness came not from seeing them overgrown and deteriorating—this often rendered them more picturesque—but from their sudden and violent destruction, which often left a big gap in the urban fabric.

At the start of my documentation I did not feel that the cities I studied were my cities or that the United States was my country. Now my images have become links that tie me to this nation. A ruined house becomes a place I could have lived in, an abandoned bakery a place I could have bought fresh bread, a derelict library a place I could have borrowed a book by Robert Louis Stevenson. And I feel I know the smell of the house, the taste of the bread, the excitement of the book.

The bakery, the house, and the derelict library are parts of my vast portfolio of other people's memories, my Smithsonian of Decline. In the 1980s I saw people peering inside a dumpster parked next door to my building, their attention drawn to the discarded hat collection of an old lady who had just died, a neighborhood character. Will all my green, red, and brown binders with their tens of thousands of slides, carefully labeled and placed in protective plastic sleeves, end up as a heap of refuse?

ACCUMULATING GLOOM: AN EDUCATION

I have sought to intensify the vision that drew me to ruins through melodies, images, and stories. I am drawn to the themes of exile, lost wars, sickness, failure, decay, and death. These works move me sometimes to tears and fill my mind with images of great power and terrible loss; yet for all their sadness they also give me pleasure.

"Terminal Island," a short story by J. G. Ballard, takes place in an abandoned atomic-weapons test facility, a desolate landscape of sand and concrete surrounded by water. The story's main character, Traven, encounters the ghosts of his dead wife and child. He finds it impossible to leave. "Visiònes de Anahuac" by Alfonso Reyes describes the life of pre-Columbian Mexico City with such vividness that I often found myself imagining "Visiònes de Gary" or "El Centro de Detroit." I imagine Gary and Detroit as the noisy, dynamic cities they once were, and see myself photographing the ghosts left behind.

I listen to the lute pieces that John Dowland composed in exile; the somber choirs of the murderer-composer Carlo Gesualdo; the grand solemnity of the "Responsorios" of the Spanish priest Tomas Luis de Victoria. Miles Davis guided me through many ghettos. Mahler's "Songs on the Death of Children" haunt me.

The poems of the Argentinean Evaristo Carriego, with their descriptions of popular barrios in Buenos Aires, speak of the importance of memories and the need to keep them alive. The morbid Colombian poet José Asuncion Silva inspired me to give expression to mystery and decay, his "music of wings." I read and reread his poem "Nocturno" about a time after death when shadows are looking for shadows and love persists.

Yunichiro Tanizaki's story "The Mother of Captain Shigemoto" introduced me to the aesthetics of a "sense of foulness," the Buddhist practice of experiencing decomposition of human bodies as a form of holiness. An essay by Carlos Monsivais entitled "Agustin Lara, el Harem Ilusorio" made me aware of the many parallels between the cult of ruins and that of prostitutes. Lara, a legendary Mexican composer and pianist (known outside the Latin world through his song "Noche de Ronda," sung by Nat King Cole), began his career in the 1920s as a teenager playing in the bordellos of Mexico City. In his works and others of the time, whores are seen as victims of circumstances or of personal weakness, fallen angels, flowers of sin; their purity is paradoxically protected by the mud in which they wallowed. Despite their degradation, diseases, and marginal status, prostitutes were idealized by men as possessing the power to intensify daily life, to renew emotions, and to provide escape from boredom.

The paintings of Giovanni Bellini, Pieter Saenraedam, Jacob van Ruisdael, Claude Monet (especially the *Rouen Cathedral* series), Edward Hopper, and Charles Sheeler taught me to photograph architecture. Eugène Atget and dozens of anonymous post-card photographers taught me to photograph streetscapes. Juan Sanchez Cotan and Walker Evans taught me to see souls in still lifes. In the paintings of Hubert Robert and Panino Panini I observed the activities that take place among ruins, the size and types of growth on their roofs, and the textures of their surfaces. Claude Lorrain showed me that Arcadia also had ruins.

I return with pleasure to the ruins, labyrinths, and prisons of Giovanni Battista Piranesi and Edgar Allan Poe. Their contemporary equivalents lie in the waiting room of Detroit's Michigan Central Railroad Station, Philadelphia's Jack Frost Sugar Refinery, and the interior of Newark's Essex County Jail, monuments that are fast disappearing. As American cities implode some of their greatest ruins, however, it is possible to imagine an America without Piranesian spaces.

12 *Big Lloyd, Tee, and friend standing among industrial ruins across from a recycling place, West Side of Chicago, 1996. They are boiling a frozen Butterball turkey given to them for Christmas dinner by a "good Samaritan."*

CHAPTER ONE

Mendelsohn's *Amerika* Revisited: "A New Reality, a New World, a New Faith"

Riding in a cart, he looked back to retain as much as possible.
Which means he knew what was needed for some ultimate moment
When he would compose from fragments a world perfect at last.
　　—Czeslaw Milosz, *The Witness of Poetry*

13 *Murphy Varnish Factory under demolition, Ironbound, Newark, 1999.*

Firemen's Insurance Headquarters at the Four Corners, Newark

14

14 *Firemen's Insurance Headquarters, Newark, 1996.*

15 *Detail of the Firemen's Insurance Headquarters, 1998.*

What would the German architect Erich Mendelsohn think, three quarters of a century after his visit, if he saw what became of the skyscrapers and industrial buildings he once admired and photographed? His idiosyncratic 1926 account of the new architecture of the United States, *Amerika*, inspires the title of this chapter.

I am fascinated by the entropic remains of the American city's golden age, by those "splendid," "arrogant," and "worldly" buildings that were meant to herald "the new, the coming thing." In the 1920s these grand buildings captured the imaginations of Erich Mendelsohn, Fritz Lang, and so many other European visitors. They symbolized America. And such grand creations continue to radiate their tremendous energy, even after being abandoned. My mission has been to account for their recent past and to articulate their meanings. I want to pay homage to their faded dreams.

According to a history of Newark, on a single day in 1915, 280,000 people were counted at the intersection of Broad and Market Streets. Local boosters of the city, predicting that Newark was growing faster than any other American municipality in the Northeast, declared the intersection the "busiest corner in America" and nicknamed it the "four corners of the world." Today a nearby Jewish deli still serves a "Four Corners plate," but the center that was the Four Corners is no more.

Newark's first skyscraper, at 786 Broad Street, was erected at this intersection in 1910. It is a slender, soaring, Beaux-Arts structure topped with elaborate ornament: a two-story Corinthian colonnade, balustrades around the perimeter of the fifteenth floor and the roof, and individual balconies at the sixteenth-floor windows. The balconies suggest that the building would serve as an observation post for magnificent views of the city and beyond, extending to the very skyline of

Manhattan. If the top three stories were separated from the rest and set atop a hill, they would resemble a small palace. The skyscraper's lightness gives it the illusion of great height. Classical decorations as well as the quality of the materials enhance its arresting beauty. Early-twentieth-century postcard manufacturers capitalized on the building's beauty and popularity, yet like many of Newark's notable buildings, 786 Broad Street is not listed in the National Register of Historic Places, nor is it included in landmark guides.

Originally, the edifice served as the headquarters for the Firemen's Insurance Company. It was a temple of commerce whose merchants moved elsewhere, and for well over a decade the building has been almost completely vacant. Today, only the ground floor has tenants: a Korean-owned business that sells gold chains, a corner eyeglass store, and an electronics outlet that promises the city's best deals on beepers. Signs of dereliction abound: the facade is dirty, a few windows are sealed with plywood, balusters are missing.

Inside the building, I could walk over the tracks my shoes left during prior visits. Along the hallway leading to the elevators hundreds of colorful plastic beeper carcasses lay in a huge cardboard box. The marble fireplace of a second-floor interior office was stuffed with used tires. A room facing Broad Street was full of empty cardboard boxes for packing electronic equipment. Throughout most of the floors, the original fine wood paneling, columns, and pilasters were covered by plywood, tall ceilings had been dropped, and the floors were covered with linoleum.

Most of the upper floors once housed city offices. Municipal Security Service was on the fourth floor, and the Parole Office, Administration, and Personnel were on the fifth. Official signs by the reception desks warned employees against selling real estate, insurance, Avon products, or leather goods during working hours. Discarded lottery tickets, brochures with pictures of new cars, and photographs of sailboats told of people's dreams. Large stacks of official documents lay in temporary storage boxes ready to be moved. The files described firings, divorces, and crimes.

As I looked through these papers, I read about the 1973 firing of Alma, a librarian who, upon arriving, had declared the

16

library's technical collection "insufficient" and the staff "inadequate"; according to the report she often came to work late. The case of Berenice also attracted my interest. It seems that this receptionist had the unfortunate propensity to lose her voice. A paper trail recorded in handwritten notes over a three-month period explained that her inability to improve the condition of her voice led to her dismissal in 1974.

I also found a report of a knife attack involving Deborah, Helen, and an unnamed man (represented only by a triangle) described in short sentences: "Grabbed arm to keep from hitting"; "Threaten to call Boss if he didn't leave"; "Went into the kitchen and got a knife"; "Reached for Mace." The account records an "annoying phone call" three weeks later.

In a former podiatrist's office on the fourth floor I found a sheet of paper with the outline of a foot bearing the name of Lucia, from Nutley, and markings indicating problem areas on her soles.

In 1981 I had visited the offices of Real Property, on the eighth and ninth floors, to pick up copies of their "Bright Future Property Auction" book—hundreds of illustrated pages of abandoned and semi-abandoned buildings, with maps showing the locations of vacant lots. A house could be bought for one hundred and fifty dollars; an abandoned factory occupying an entire block for five hundred dollars; a still-occupied, three-story building for three thousand dollars; a fourteen-story building for ten thousand dollars; a vacant lot for seventy-five dollars. It seemed incredible that, in 1915, land at the Four Corners sold at five thousand dollars per square foot.

Near the sixteenth floor, in a former lawyer's office, were piles of divorce records. A 1972 document awarded the husband, John, unlimited visitation rights provided that he give "at least twenty-four hours notice of intention to visit." He was ordered to pay twenty dollars per child per week.

The flapping wings of startled pigeons crashing against windows announce the upper floors. An increasing sense of isolation accompanies the ascent. The presence of 786 Broad Street becomes overwhelming. One hundred and fifty feet and sixteen floors separate a visitor from the nearest human being.

A climb up the rusted iron ladder that

16 *Office, Firemen's Insurance Headquarters, 1996.*

17 *Ground floor, facing Broad Street, Firemen's Insurance Headquarters, 1998. A case of "oversigning."*

leads to the roof over the elevator machinery presents an extraordinary view out toward the east and north. Visible are college campuses and a new downtown, its glassy boxes linked to Penn Station by above-ground connectors that look like giant dark hoses. To the west are new townhouses, which, like other new buildings, announce Newark's "renaissance." To the west along Springfield Avenue is another architectural glory of Newark: the Essex County Courthouse, by the Beaux-Arts architect Cass Gilbert. Across the street, to the south, the flight of a tiny falcon leads the eye toward the top of a column of the Kinney Building, yet another derelict beauty. On the roof, the city's sounds seem remote. Above is nothing but sky.

In the sixteenth-floor lobby I found tools and a flashlight, indicating that elevator mechanics had recently been bringing life back to the building. But things go on as before. Newark's first skyscraper continues to collect dust and serve as a retail outlet for beepers and gold chains.

The building is a time capsule that candidly and vividly reveals more about Newark and its inhabitants during the past three decades than any official source. Because these fragments are unselfconscious documents, not processed for public consumption, they provide invaluable testimony about their times.

In the past my heavy camera bag made me look like an elevator mechanic, which gave me easy access to the building. Now visitors need to get permission from the rental agent, and there are locks, barbed wire, and iron plates barring the way. Maybe someday someone with the passion to tell the recent story of Newark will break in and "read" this building.

I saw the former Firemen's Insurance Headquarters as a mountaintop, a cher-ished piece of America, a place to learn about the endurance and frailties of people and to find tranquillity. I would come out of this magnificent building feeling fortified by my encounters with living ghosts and eager to photograph and write about the grandiose decline of urban America.

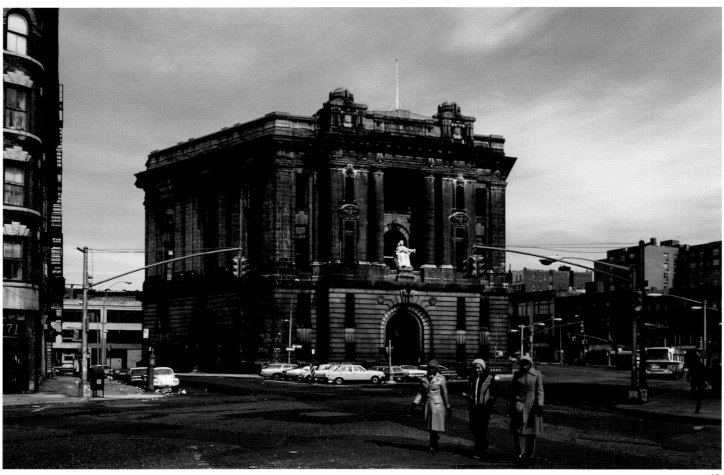

Bronx Borough Courthouse: A Gray Eminence

The former Bronx Borough Courthouse, a gray Beaux-Arts building designed by Alexander Garvin, sits on an island at 161st Street in the heart of the South Bronx. Grand remarks by County Counselor Louis Van Doren accompanied its inauguration in 1914: "May this Courthouse and this chamber be from now on the center from which shall radiate over this community Justice and Equity." Passengers traveling on the Third Avenue Elevated could look at the statue of Justice at the second-story level, and Justice, unblindfolded, would look back. In 1978, the building was closed, and a year later it was declared a city landmark.

The courthouse exterior, darkened by layers of grime, is gritty and severe. Mayor Edward Koch's order to seal the building in the mid-1980s only increased my desire to see the interior, and I have often circled the perimeter, regretting my missed chances to get inside. Others took their opportunities before the building was sealed; the superintendent of a nearby building remembered seeing people walk off with pieces of marble, chandeliers, hand-painted windows—even a brass eagle.

Yolanda Garcia, of a local grassroots group, "Nos Quedamos" (We Stay), said that the lobby's rotunda is large enough for a production of *Phantom of the Opera*. When I asked her if the building would survive, she answered, "They can't demolish it; it is a landmark of the city." She dismissed the idea of arson: "If people had wanted to burn it, they would have a long time ago." Garcia envisions a market outside and community

facilities inside, but it is unlikely that rehabilitation will come soon.

It would cost forty-three million dollars
to remove the asbestos and restore the
courthouse, a huge amount for a building in
the South Bronx. The old landmark is isolated. The area has only recently seen some
rebuilding. Bernd Zimmerman of the Bronx
Borough President's Office told me that he
appreciated its "ruined" look but that he
thought the building should be stabilized
and "made habitable as a ruin." Such a com-
bination, he acknowledged, is a long shot.

18 *Bronx Borough Courthouse,
left vacant and open, Bronx,
1980.*

19 *Bronx Borough Courthouse,
1996.*

20

20 *Bronx Borough Courthouse, sealed, 1997.*

21 *Allegorical figure of Justice, Bronx Borough Courthouse, 1999. The figure was sculpted from Tennessee marble by French artist J. E. Roine.*

21

Packard Automobile Plant, Detroit

22

22 *Packard Automobile Plant (now Motor City Industrial Park), Detroit, 1991.*

The first structures of the Packard Plant in Detroit were designed in 1903 by the distinguished architect Albert Kahn. Packard grew until the end of World War II, when Rolls-Royce airplane engines were made there. The firm had a reputation for technological leadership. Their factories demonstrated advanced design: large windows, rational floor plans, early use of air conditioning, soundproofing, and fluorescent light. In 1956, however, the plant stopped producing automobiles.

By the time of my first visit in 1987, the complex had been renamed Motor City Industrial Park. Today the buildings are mostly empty; small tenants occupy a tiny fraction of the available space. A mere five maintenance men work in the half-mile-long, three-and-a-half-million-square-foot plant. A sign in the parking lot warns "Construction Zone" and advises parking at least ten feet from the nearby building. But there is no construction going on; "Falling Debris" would be more accurate.

The owner of a garage-door-repair company finds the former plant a convenient place for his business. Its location is adjacent to all the expressways and there are plenty of parking spaces. Among the other tenants are a laundry with several delivery trucks, small garages where a lone mechanic is sometimes seen doing body work, a repair shop for electrical equipment, a paper recycling facility, and a bakery called Economy Cookies. The park rents storage space for boats and cars. One tenant refurbishes old shoes, clothes, and stuffed animals to sell in Third World countries.

23

24

Illegal parties known as "raves" are staged inside the buildings. Invitation is by word of mouth, and the locations vary to avoid police raids. The party promoters provide the place, music, drinks, and bouncers, and guests pay about thirty dollars each to attend. Usually the organizers supply a set of old refrigerators stocked with beer. The partygoers help themselves. Techno, which originated in Detroit, is the music of choice.

A large sign on the plant's roof announces "Splatt Ball City, Stress Free Capital of the World" and the "World's Largest Indoor Paint Ball Field." Typically, a group of thirty or forty people, mostly men, rents a section of the plant to play war games with paint-pellet guns. As the receptionist explains: "They set up a flag there, then they try to capture it. Once you get the flag the game is over." The game is played indoors in winter and outdoors in summer. At the Packard Plant people don't have to worry about damaging the walls. Peter, a planning student who likes the game, thinks that playing inside a decrepit building adds to its attraction. "It's not the same as playing out in the cornfields," he says. "It's out of a video game, out of *Blade Runner.*"

The fragmented use of this vast Piranesian space is reminiscent of Rome during the Middle Ages. As the architectural historian Spiro Kostof has written, "In Rome the great theaters, the stadiums, the baths, the public colonnades were cut up into little pieces. These structures were too expensive to keep, and culturally they were not compatible with the new religion of Christianity."

When speaking to the property manager, I called Packard a ruin and commented on the eerie emptiness of its buildings. He angrily responded that five hundred people work there—for ninety-seven tenants occupying 35 percent of the space. He added that the complex, work of the great Albert Kahn,

23 *An interior road inside the Packard Plant, 1993.*

24 *Fourth floor of the Packard Plant, 1998. Such spaces are now used for paint-gun battles and raves.*

25 *Disabled truck, now one of the props for the war games played inside the Packard Plant, 1998.*

26

was no more a ruin than the Empire State Building or the Statue of Liberty. Like them, all it needed was to be fixed. His notion of the building's "stability," however, is not likely to be shared by more dispassionate observers.

I drove my rented car, lights on, for several hundred yards on the third floor of the complex. The plant's windows are boarded up, creating the effect of a tunnel, and its ground is covered with planks, some of which are missing. I suddenly realized that I might hit a hole and drop down a couple of levels. I quickly turned around toward downtown Detroit, hoping that the city would never get the fifteen or twenty million dollars it will need to raze this wonderful old plant.

27

28

26 *View from the roof, Packard Plant, 1998.*

27 *Entrance to a techno music enterprise at the Packard Plant, 1998. The graphics look like a cross between the Korean alphabet and computer circuitry.*

28 *A 1948 Packard, Bell, California, 1997.*

RCA Victor's "Nipper" Building, Camden: "The Little Dog in the Sky"

29

29 *Building 17, RCA Victor plant, Camden, 1997.*

30 *RCA Victor's "Nipper Tower," 1997.*

31 *Floor of an RCA Victor building after fire, 1997.*

RCA Victor no longer exists. Building 17 is now the property of the city of Camden and lies empty. Nevertheless, its four-story tower still contains enormous fourteen-foot-diameter stained-glass medallions. They depict a fox terrier named Nipper—the familiar symbol of the Victor Talking Machine Company and, later, of RCA Victor—who continues to listen to "His Master's Voice" on a gramophone. Dubbed the "Nipper Building" after the listening dog, Building 17 is no longer lit up at night, and many of the Nipper windows have been shattered by vandals.

Once the mile of frontage on both sides of the Delaware River bordering the downtowns of Philadelphia and Camden was home to many large factories. The area was then billed the "Workshop of the World."

The historian Robert Fishman urged me to visit Camden's RCA buildings—"they're blowing them up," he claimed.

So I went to Camden to see the "Radio Capital of the World." The six-to-eight-story RCA buildings are basic industrial forms, with large windows and elevators of the kind built during the first quarter of the century. More radios were produced within these massive structures than anywhere else in the world. The country's music industry began here; Enrico Caruso and Louis Armstrong recorded in those buildings. Some of my favorite tango records bear the RCA label. At its peak, during World War II, it employed thirteen thousand workers.

An old letter "to all Union Members" found on the ground floor of one of the buildings announces that the plant will be permanently shut down between Christmas and New Year's 1986–87. RCA and its successors owned the buildings until 1993, when the Camden Redevelopment Agency took over.

Accounts of the building's dereliction and possible demise are usually followed by reassurances that the original stained-glass windows depicting dog and gramophone have been preserved: one at the Camden County Historic Society, another at the Smithsonian, and two others at local universities. But the windows by themselves mean very little; their allure comes from their position in the tower. The local development agency, Cooper's Ferry, is now dreaming of establishing a museum of the history of sound in Building 17. As a start the organization is struggling to preserve Building 17 and has replaced the broken windows with new ones. John Grady, an officer with the organization, calls them "one of the most recognizable images in America."

During my visit in 1998, I reached the tower room via a spiral staircase, rusted and missing rungs. There I saw that a new icon had emerged from the vandalized windows: the sight of Nipper, shattered by stones, bullets, and bottles, was a surprise. The image shone precariously in its own light-filled room.

30

31

Jack Frost Sugar Refinery, Philadelphia: The Piranesian Lost

32

Across the river from RCA Victor, north of the Ben Franklin Bridge, is the old Jack Frost plant. In 1960 it was the world's largest sugar refinery, with 1,200 employees. The 1937 WPA guide to Philadelphia described the early-twentieth-century complex as a "strangely shaped geometrical brick mass, from which protrude at fantastic angles a variety of tanks and metal pipes." Closed since 1981, the buildings have stood in the way of waterfront development. One was partly demolished recently. A demolition company from Iowa was hired to level a ten-story 1901 building. I raced from New York to get there by 8:00 AM, only to find that the implosion had been canceled. "They ran some tests; not enough explosives," said a security guard. I stood outside as others arrived and received the same news. "Come back next Sunday," we were told. The block-long building's entrails were showing. Behind its dark, dirty, brown-brick walls and windows covered with bright white sheets,

asbestos was being removed. When I tried to go inside the guard blocked my way.

James Dickinson, a sociologist, witnessed the rescheduled demolition in my stead and called to give me the score: "Building four, people zero... The dynamite exploded, but it wasn't enough... The building is still up. They're trying to pull it down with ropes... If it falls unexpectedly, a cloud of dust will envelop I-95, causing all kinds of accidents; they'll have to close the road."

Local television reporters on the site interviewed former workers. An electrician volunteered an explanation of the demolition difficulties; the structure had thick concrete floors and was built with "Drummond steel," a mythical and now-forgotten product. Another explained that this heavy-duty construction technique was necessary because sugar is highly combustible and tends to explode. Onlookers began to cheer for the building; its resilience gave it a new dignity. Former

workers proudly remembered that they once had solid jobs and solid lives in this solid place. After much pulling and tugging at the central beam with the largest bulldozers in the metropolitan area, the building fell that night. The neighborhood rumor was that the land would be used for a hotel or perhaps a casino.

How could this leftover from history have fit into the new Philadelphia? The dark bricks, gaping holes, and smokestack could have been left standing; the structure could have been illuminated at night with dark reds and intense blues; a casino could have been built inside the old refinery. It could have become the world's most sinister gambling place, the dark and foreboding Jack Frost Casino—a gritty, post-urban answer to Las Vegas, to Disney, to Atlantic City, and to the Pompidou Center in Paris.

I repeat to myself the shallow litanies I once read in a special 1997 issue of the *New York Times Magazine* entitled "How the

33

34

35

32 *Jack Frost Sugar Refinery, North Philadelphia, July 1997.*

33 *Jack Frost Refinery, October 1997.*

34 *Jack Frost Refinery, September 1997.*

35 *Detail of the Cave, a nightclub near the Jack Frost Refinery, North Philadelphia, 1997. Its decor matches the rusted cores of surrounding buildings.*

World Sees Us": "America sits on the top"… "We live in an American age"…"By adapting, competing and improving"… "Eighty percent say that the future belongs to the American system." The images of the Jack Frost plant, as it resists gravity, and RCA's Nipper, still a magnificent American icon, give me hope.

American Brewery, Baltimore: "A Magical Storybook Castle"

The red-brick structure of the American Brewery, designed by Charles Stoll in 1887, looms above Baltimore's surrounding row houses, a warm, protective, but sometimes unsettling presence. The building is memorable for its tower, reminiscent of Darth Vader's helmet, its lack of symmetry, and its large scale in relation to the low-rise neighborhood.

One of the city's thirty-three breweries, it was closed and simultaneously placed on the National Register of Historic Places in 1973. In 1975 the structure was recognized as "one of the finest surviving American examples of the Teutonic brewery style." In front was a twelve-foot pewter statue of the mythical King Gambrinus of Flanders, the putative inventor of beer, holding a mug of beer in his upraised hand, toasting passersby for almost a century. The statue went to the

Smithsonian in 1976 and remains there on permanent loan.

A 1998 newspaper editorial declared the brewery the "prime example" of a notable structure likely to be destroyed. During a visit that year, I saw a bulldozer clearing houses and razing trees on the next block. The alleys alongside the vacant structure were littered with discarded shoes. Hopes for the building's rehabilitation are tempered by its location: the heart of East Baltimore, a ghetto with a thriving drug trade.

A 1973 article in the *Evening Sun* describes the building as a "peculiar structure of towers, shadowy eaves and arched brick windows...It is perhaps the most eccentric and interesting building in Baltimore. For such a place surely there must be a purpose—as a museum, a school, a theater. If it falls victim to the

36

wrecker's ball, as the beer within fell victim
to the deterioration of popular taste,
Baltimore will be twice the loser."

The Victorian fantasy architecture of
the American Brewery is delightful. It is,
in the words of the 1973 article, a "temple
of Bacchus," a "Germanic pagoda," with an
asymmetrical front and a curious mixture
of Romanesque and Queen Anne ornament. Had the statue been kept in situ,
King Gambrinus and Baltimore's beer
might have been able to ensure the building's long-term survival.

36 *American Brewery,
Baltimore, 1998. View along
North Gay Street.*

37 *American Brewery, 1998.*

38

38 *Detail of the roof of the American Brewery, 1998.*

39 *American Brewery, view from behind, 1998.*

40 *Derelict gas pump at the American Brewery, 1999.*

39

An Alternative View of the Detroit Skyline

41

42

The common view of the Detroit skyline, the one visible from Metro Airport, at postcard stands, and in official publications, is the view toward the north across the Detroit River from Windsor, Canada. The city rises above a wide body of water, a wall of skyscrapers dominated on the right by the Renaissance Center, the tallest of them all. Cargo ships and pleasure boats move slowly across the water.

The impression is of a calm, modern, and prosperous city.

I prefer the view from the roof of Harbor Light, a drug treatment facility on Park Avenue, immediately north of downtown. Empty lots and the Fisher Freeway replace the river. A different set of skyscrapers, those built before the Great Depression, emerges in the distance. These are tall, mostly vacant, and look much like

Hugh Ferriss's disenchanted mountains. Seen from the roof, the diminutive people below, crossing the empty lots or walking down the middle of Park Avenue, impart grandeur to the scene. These tiny figures of homeless people, alcoholics, addicts, and prostitutes who live in the Cass Corridor are the modern-day equivalents of the shepherds depicted among the ruins of antiquity by painters like Claude and Piranesi.

43

41 *Detroit skyline, 1991.*

42 *Fireworks over Detroit skyline, 1996.*

43 *Detroit skyline, 1997.*

44 *Detroit skyline, 1998.*

44

J. L. Hudson's Department Store: The Hulk that Blotted Out the Sun

"This is the largest building that has ever been shot in the world," said Roger Homrich, the president of one of the demolition companies handling the job. From 1911 until it closed in 1983, Hudson's was the center of downtown Detroit's life. The building was twenty-five stories tall, employed twelve thousand people, used 350 olive-green delivery vans, and received one hundred thousand shoppers a day. The flagpole atop its 1928 tower seemed taller than any tree in Michigan.

When it closed, Hudson's became known as a "mere ghost of an era past," a dark and highly visible reminder of the decline of downtown. The derelict structure was blamed for "strangling downtown's resurgence." Mayor Dennis Archer described it as a "millstone hanging around Detroit's neck." As the building imploded (at the cost of twelve million dollars), he proclaimed: "Let the future begin." "Watching the sun shine over that block is just wonderful," added Beth DunCombe, the president of Detroit's Economic Growth Corporation.

With the grand old building gone, city officials are now free to envision "airy office buildings and a world-class hotel, specialty shops and a department store, cafes and fine restaurants" rising on the site. John Mogk, professor of urban development law at Wayne State University, sounded doubtful that these developments would take place soon: "If there were a considerable level of investor interest, projects would be materializing as in other major cities, and the fact [that] they're not indicates that the climate is still marginal."

After demolition, Hudson's bricks were guarded by the police and then sold for five dollars apiece to lines of people. One man wanted to build Hudson's bricks into his new home. Another planned to use a brick as a doorstop. Yet another wanted to place a brick from the store on the grave of his father-in-law, who had been a Hudson's employee for forty-five years.

45

46

47

45 *J. L. Hudson's Department Store, Detroit, 1995.*

46 *Hudson's Department Store, January 1997.*

47 *Site of Hudson's Department Store, December, 1998. After the building's demolition, Canada and the Detroit River became visible.*

Four Vacant Skyscrapers

48

Depending on how you see it, the former Book-Cadillac Hotel either needs to be demolished or is a likely place to receive divine revelation. By 1993, Ken Dobson, then the city council's vice president, had given up on the derelict hotel, calling it a "nuisance." He needed four and a half million dollars to raze it. But to the anonymous man who clocks the number of divine appearances in downtown Detroit with a black felt-tip, the ruined hotel is a favorite spot. Indeed, with its Corinthian pilasters, sculpted lions and historical figures, and tattered mauve awnings on the side windows (installed in 1980 when Detroit hosted the Republican Convention), the Book-Cadillac seems more fit for the Divinity than useful to advanced capitalism.

Once, when I wanted to go inside to see the famous "Venetian" and "Florentine" rooms, a guard at a side entrance, where a machete was hanging from the wall, told me: "You can't go in. It belongs to the Federal Government."

Likewise, I was barred from entering the empty Metropolitan Building by a state employee, who told me that it was contaminated. I did manage to get a view of it from the top of a nearby skyscraper. Rising from the facade is a tower decorated with neo-Tudor visors and shields. Behind the tower the roof steps down, forming a terrace upon which grow the tallest trees on any Detroit skyscraper.

48 *Book-Cadillac Hotel, Detroit, 1998. Designed by Louis Kamper and built in 1924 in the Italian Renaissance style as Detroit's premier hotel, the building hosted guests including Presidents Truman, Eisenhower, Johnson, and Kennedy. The Book-Cadillac was closed in*

1979; the facade was given a facelift for the Republican National Convention in 1980. Due to lack of funds for demolition, the building still stands.

49 *Side view of the Book-Cadillac Hotel, 1996.*

49

I have often walked around the Kales Building looking for an opening, hoping to be as lucky as my friend Garrick, who once made it to the top floor and visited the former president's office of the Kresge Company.

On the other hand, I have had easy access to the thirty-five-story David Broderick Tower of 1928, prominently situated on the southeast corner of Grand Circus Park and Woodward Avenue. Apparently, the bottle-shaped building is too clumsy to be mentioned in the local AIA guide. Nor does it appear in the more voluminous guide *Buildings of Detroit*.

The entry hall is adorned with a wallpaper frieze of Roman ruins, including an overgrown triumphal arch and broken columns, and populated by the figures of *banditti*. Ironically the lobby's decorators would never have predicted that this building was destined to be among the first skyscrapers in the world to undergo ruination. It was with great pride and confidence that the city's wealthy entrepreneurs selected classical forms and imagery to decorate the structure.

The penthouse on the thirty-fifth floor provides a 360-degree view of downtown. From a balcony the view encompasses the Detroit River, a thin blue line in the distance, with Windsor, Ontario, on its other side. From another balcony the city expands endlessly northward. From the once elegant private bar, the city reappears in a tinted, mural-size panoramic photograph of downtown. Another large-scale mural presents a black-and-white nighttime view of the building from Grand Circus Park, its magnificent fountain splashing in the foreground. The mural showcases the David Broderick in all its glory, the tall shaft of the building emerging like a rocket launched from a halo of light. Apparently the residents enjoyed watching and being watched; a sofa next to a marble fireplace in the ballroom faces a picture window.

This once luxurious showplace is perhaps

50

50 *Kales Building, Detroit, 1995. Designed by architect Albert Kahn as the Kresge Company Headquarters, the skyscraper was erected in 1914.*

Closed in 1986, it is included on Detroit's Grand Circus Park National Register Historic District.

more interesting now than it was in its heyday. Its emptiness is exhilarating, but no one pays it any heed. The rooms contain a random assortment of remains: large mirrors, a mattress, and, on the floor, a poster of a rocky beach with the saying, attributed to Martin Buber, "All Real Living Is Meeting."

For thirty years Jessie Willie Sr. has been the David Broderick Tower's caretaker and my guide to the building. When he started he had a staff of nine. Now he is alone. When he encountered a big pile of plaster fallen from the ceiling of the thirty-fourth floor, Jessie asked, "How did that shit fall?" Recently the present owner invited nearly a hundred people to watch fireworks from the roof, and they left behind many empty bottles and cans. In his early eighties, Jessie can hardly walk. His back hurts, and he has trouble getting up the stairs to the roof. Picking up these bottles is, for him, an impossible task, so he just looks at them and gets angry at the people who dumped them.

Jessie is probably the last person to identify with this proud tower. He must feel left behind. "There is nothing wrong with this building," he told me, and to prove it, he turned on lights and opened windows and closets. On the way down, when I expressed a mild concern that we might get stuck in the elevator, he made it run fast, proudly explaining that it could go even faster. Yet I feel that Jessie has given up trying to convince people of the building's soundness. I imagine him carrying on a sort of ritual dialogue with the building: "What's wrong? Why don't they like us anymore?"

Jessie's plight reminded Chicago historian Tim Samuelson of that of the *Titanic*'s second officer, the one who stayed onboard and miraculously survived being swept overboard by the waves. When later asked when he left the ship, he answered, "I never left the ship; the ship left me."

51

51 *Metropolitan Building, Detroit, 1998. Erected in 1925 by Weston and Ellington, architects, the building was the jewelry center of Detroit until it closed in 1977. On April 5, 1925, the* Detroit News *called it a "strikingly impressive building," a "million-dollar Gothic structure and a worthy addition to the Detroit skyline."*

52 *The top of the David
Broderick Tower, Detroit, 1998.*

53 *Jessie Willie Sr., the building's
eighty-one-year-old caretaker, in
the bar of what was the penthouse
apartment in the David Broderick
Tower, 1995.*

52

53

Michigan Central Railroad Station: The Piranesian Preserved

I have photographed the former Michigan Central Railroad Station at least twice a year for eight years, but I refrained from going inside until 1995. The station, a huge, austere, neoclassical building erected in 1913 by Warren & Wetmore on the model of the Baths of Caracalla, is now derelict, isolated: a menacing presence. At the entrance someone has written "Isa 23"—"Howl, ye ships of Tarshish; for it is laid waste, so that there is no house, no entering in" (Isaiah 23).

Dwarfed by the enormous entrance, I found myself dazzled, surrounded by patches of illumination and darkness in the middle of an extraordinary interior. Returning to this cavernous space many times, I am always awed by its silence. Three separate vaults, supported by

columns, articulate the main hall, which is lit by three large, iron-frame windows facing north. On sunny days lunettes at both ends of the station bring in floods of light.

During the past eight years at Michigan Central, increasing numbers of window panes have been broken; trees and bushes growing wildly in front of the building were cut; the iron roof looks more rusted. On one of my visits I saw a small bulldozer clearing benches in the waiting room and removing pieces of glass and plaster from the floor, leaving an unobstructed experience of space.

Grand Central Station in New York City, also the work of Warren & Wetmore and erected the same year as Michigan Central, recently underwent a two-hundred-million-dollar restoration. I could not help contrasting these two great train stations, one celebrated as the "palace of all train stations," a triumph of historic preservation, the other forgotten or viewed as a disgrace. Grand Central is full of people rushing, their steps and voices resonating through the main vault of the building. In Detroit nothing arrives or leaves from the former station; only the imagination travels. There are no loudspeakers announcing departures and arrivals, no footsteps reverberating on the walls. With half a million men and women passing through the New York landmark in one day, a visitor feels safe, while in the Detroit station a rare encounter with a person is fraught with danger. The new Grand Central has elegant shops and restaurants, and its halls are lit by dozens of golden chandeliers. Nothing is for sale in Detroit's former station, and its interior is lit by the sun, the moon, and the occasional squatter's fire.

The former depot has the power to challenge artists. Of the several examples of poetry, graffiti, and sculpture I have seen in the station, the most powerful give me a feeling of horror. On a freezing Christmas Day in 1998 I saw a tiny human figure framed by a steel arch. The sun shone on it from behind as I approached the western end of the old building. It was a sculptural armature resembling a standing woman frozen in place. When I went to see the figure up close, I saw that it was a maquette, probably from an art school. It was in open stride with its head turned down and its handless arms loose at its sides. Painted light blue, it was an anonymous embodiment of defeat.

Declining cities could learn from the Middle Ages. Michigan Central Station and a few dozen surrounding acres of old parking lots and railroad tracks should be turned into an abbey or monastery. Government or foundation money would help a group of monks to stabilize the ruin and establish living quarters in it. I envision local farmers willingly cooperating, assisting the monks in setting up their farm, chicken coops, and barnyards. I see strawberries growing between the rails along the train tracks; I see lambs and cattle grazing

55

54 *Michigan Central Railroad Station, Detroit, 1998.*

55 *Entrance, Michigan Central, 1998.*

on the overgrown parking lots and goats on the roof and staring out the windows. I cannot wait to eat Michigan Central brand eggs, butter, chicken, tomatoes, and strawberries. I would even expect an enterprising order of monks to set up a micro-brewery and market their own brand of jam.

Neighboring schoolchildren coming to help with the farm would be treated to a healthy meal and given aid with their homework. At the end of the day the monks would gather and sing in the main hall. The sublime space of Michigan Central Station would go on decaying a little but would also support life, becoming a ruin while contributing to the city's economic development and paying taxes. Michigan Central would bring visitors from all over the world to Detroit. Motown would become the "city where the Middle Ages work." Who knows? Perhaps another order of monks could be convinced to set up a community at the former Packard Plant.

56 *Lobby, Michigan Central, 1997.*

57 *"Catfish," a three-year resident of Michigan Central, 1998.*

58 *Androgynous six-foot-tall face spray-painted on the second floor of Michigan Central, 1998.*

59 *Sculptural armature left on the west side of Michigan Central, 1998.*

57

58

59

The Disappearance of Rickel Malt

Detroit's Eastern Market and the German neighborhood just east of it used to be cohesive and dynamic. The wholesale malt supplier Rickel Malt, established in 1875, played a key role. Saint Joseph's Church, across the street, is a landmark.

Rickel Malt supplied the smaller breweries in Detroit. One of them was Goebel, next to the church, and two others, E & B and National Bohemian, were nearby. As the wholesale malt business lost its market, they all closed down and disappeared. Rickel was active until the early 1960s.

Now the old German neighborhood is decimated, but the underground railroad tracks that connected Rickel Malt to its silos are still visible. These are precisely the sort of structures that inspired Le Corbusier's comments in *Towards a New Architecture* (1923): *"Thus we have the American grain elevators and factories, the magnificent* FIRST-FRUITS *of the new age.* THE AMERICAN ENGINEERS OVER-WHELM WITH THEIR CALCULATIONS OUR EXPIRING ARCHITECTURE.*"*

60

61

60 *Rickel Malt Brewery, Detroit, 1994.*

61 *Rickel Malt Brewery replaced by clouds, 1998.*

The Disinherited Mansions of Brush Park

62

62 *Brush Park along John R. Street, Detroit, 1998. The city skyline contrasts with the cluster of ruined Victorian houses.*

In the Brush Park section of Detroit, a handful of derelict castles and Victorian mansions sit on fifty-foot lots in splendid isolation—as if on a spacious campus. These houses are all that survive of a once upper-class neighborhood. Developed in the last quarter of the nineteenth century on an old farm immediately north of downtown Detroit, the nearly one hundred family houses were once regarded as among the most beautiful examples of American domestic architecture. In 1998 only about fifteen of these homes were still maintained. Many others stood vacant and deteriorating, and still others had disappeared entirely. Among the remaining mansions, some are on the Woodward East National Register of Historic Places, and others are on the state register. The area was designated a local historic district in 1980.

Brush Park was the most fashionable neighborhood in Detroit. During its heyday, it was a favorite among the creators of the city's new wealth: manufacturers, merchants, lawyers, and land speculators. "Naturally, creators of this wealth needed substantial residences to reflect their own importance," reported *The Antique Collector* in May 1988. Residents were board members of churches and hospitals, philanthropists, a collector of violins, a jurist who wrote a book on the political history of Michigan, and even an engineer who surveyed the Panama Canal.

At the beginning of the twentieth century, Brush Park began a decline that continues to this day. First, its wealthiest

residents left for the larger houses in newly developed neighborhoods such as Boston-Edison to the north and Indian Village to the east. The population increased dramatically as the miniature castles and palaces were divided into flats and rooming houses for factory workers. Several apartment buildings were constructed during the century's first two decades, further increasing the neighborhood's density.

The first threat to the architectural integrity of the mansions was posed by growth between 1880 and 1920. Mechanics and inventors involved with the auto industry maintained their shops in extensive rear additions to their homes. Hardware stores, gas stations, restaurants, laundries, beauty salons, storage warehouses, and small groceries sprung up. One dwelling became the Lewis School for Stammerers; the coach house of the Ransom Gillis house on Alfred Street turned into the first home of Pewabic

Pottery; the Victor Screw Works was founded behind a house on Winder Street.

Decline accelerated after the riots of 1967 and the ensuing white flight to the suburbs. New businesses came to the area, like the City Cab Company, with its garage and parking lot. The back extensions of the houses along Alfred Street became illegal drug markets. Vacant houses were used as shooting galleries and were inhabited by squatters. In 1985 *Wall Street Journal* writer Raymond Sokolov described Alfred Street as a place where "disinherited mansions with mansard and slate roofs alternate with vacant lots" and "junkies prowl the sidewalks." In 1988, Brush Park had the fifth poorest zip-code district in the nation.

During the late 1970s and early 1980s many of the houses were demolished to make room for infill housing as part of a federally funded program connected to the American Bicentennial. The idea was to

63 *Brush Park with the Frost house in the foreground, 1987.*

64 *The Frost house stripped bare, 1994.*

65 *The Frost house being boarded up just before demolition, 1997.*

64

65

give jobs to the unemployed while restoring the mansions and building houses for low-income residents. The program failed in all three respects. Without skilled carpenters and preservation specialists it could not restore the inside of the houses, fix roofs, or repair ornamentation. Activities were limited to demolition, rebuilding sidewalks, replacing steps, and doing minor carpentry. The infill housing was never built.

The program did have unintended consequences, however. By demolishing the area's abandoned dwellings and sparing the most notable structures, it left the latter "alone in the landscape, lonely beacons on a sea of rubble," as journalist Peter Waldmeir described the situation. The remaining mansions were isolated amid overgrown vegetation, where they were set off like extraordinary jewels—gems of devastation.

Scavengers vandalized the houses and continue to do so. Brass fixtures and marble fireplaces were stolen long ago. Thieves now chisel away the decorative stonework, the bricks, and even the plywood used to seal the houses. "Things got bad last year," said Bill Atwood, a six-year resident of nearby Edmond Place, in 1998. He spoke of finding fragments of lintels strewn all over the ground. "These are not professional strippers. They miscalculate; they don't know these stones weigh two hundred pounds."

I have followed the dissolution of these mansions for over a decade. In 1997, upon hearing that the Frost house would be demolished in three weeks, neighborhood people grew excited: "If I were you I would come early and get all of that carved stone"; "I don't know how I am going to get all that slate but I want it bad." Soon even the beauty of the houses as ruins will be gone. In the words of Randy Hunter, a Brush Park homeowner, "my impression is that it is all coming down...all coming down."

67

66 *Site of the Frost house, Detroit, 1997.*

67 *Brush Park, 1987. The Ransom Gillis house, on the left, was built in 1876 by Brush & Mason for a founder of Edson, Moore & Co., a large dry-goods firm.*

69

70

68 *Tower detail of the Ransom Gillis house, 1998.*

69 *Ransom Gillis house, 1993.*

70 *Ransom Gillis house, January 1997.*

71 *Ransom Gillis house, 1997.*

71

72

72 *Houses on Alfred Street, Brush Park, 1987. This row of four Second Empire townhouses was built in 1883.*

73 *Row houses on Alfred Street, 1995. People line up at Christmas to receive donated clothes.*

74 *Row houses on Alfred Street, 1998.*

75 *Row houses on Alfred Street, 1998.*

73

75

CHAPTER TWO

Modest Ruins

Another One Dead & Gone
    —Graffiti on the wall of a Chicago Housing Authority building, 1998

76 *Collapsed house on the East Side of Detroit, 1998.*

East New York from the L Train, 1978–1998: Space . . . Space . . . Space

I have never been able to forget the sensation of walking through New York City's devastated neighborhoods in the late 1970s and early 1980s and seeing the newly charred buildings, piles of bricks, and collapsing walls. Nationally, these scenes were unprecedented. People did not know how to explain the catastrophe that was before their eyes, yet they recognized the great magnitude of what they saw. These apocalyptic places obliterated the separation between me and my physical surroundings, producing the hallucinatory feeling that I could project my consciousness as far as the eye could see, that I could breathe blocks away from my body and see behind my back.

For two decades I have observed a two-block-long strip that borders Sutter Avenue along Brooklyn's L subway line. I first visited East New York to see the last remnants of a crumbling neighborhood once called Little Pittsburgh. Russians, Poles, Ukrainians, and Germans had lived there, and it had been the birthplace of George Gershwin and Danny Kaye. During the 1970s, the population of this area was reduced to one-tenth of its former size, a cataclysmic change. *New York Times* reporter Francis X. Clines compared what was happening to the effect of a virus that attacks the body's material order. "What next?" I asked myself.

During periodic returns to the Sutter Avenue stop, I've noticed that the former synagogue, Chevra Sphard of Perry Slaw, bears a sign that reads "La Sinagoga"; but on the roof someone has painted the words "Cristo Viene." The Premier Theater, the largest structure in the area, was demolished, and a florist moved next door only to be closed and subsequently leveled. Two blocks to the east, a defiant homeowner painted his brick row house green and white—a symbol of hope. In the distance, to the east of Sutter Avenue, is Unity Plaza, one of the city's worst housing projects. The only building that has been erected since 1978 is a homeless shelter. For

77

78

79

80

a few years the empty land was used as a ball field. It is now one of the city's car pounds. The few trees growing in the area are behind bars, inside the shelter's fenced compound.

81

82

83

"Little Beirut," Harlem

Ibo Balton of Harlem's division of Housing Preservation and Development, describes an entire residential block without residents: "We call that block 'Little Beirut.' It is the most devastated block of Harlem today. The tenements in that block are more than one hundred years old; they don't have the amenities associated with modern life. We are waiting for money to do the entire block with new buildings." In 1988 I photographed the block bounded by Madison Avenue, 131st Street, Park Avenue, and 132nd Street and was surprised to discover that the area had at one time about two thousand residents. By 1988, however, just one building was occupied, and only occasional squatters lived in the rest. A decade later, after the largest rebuilding program in the city's history, the block was completely empty. I have heard at least two commissioners of housing publicly declare that New York City has run out of vacant buildings to fix. What was I seeing, then?

The Sanborn map of Manhattan indicates lots for twenty-seven buildings in the block. Yet on my last visit there were only thirteen, all of them derelict buildings, with more than 250 abandoned apartments—no residents. The block has two small grocery stores, a storefront church, and three parking lots. The residents of neighboring blocks were somewhat hopeful about the future. They had seen buildings across Madison Avenue rehabilitated, and they expected this desolate block to be fixed, too. It was with a mixture of hope and irony that someone told me, "The city has a plan, but they are in no hurry." When I called one of the block's absentee landlords, I received a rather cryptic response from his lawyer: "I don't own property there; our client does. He does not know anything about it. I know even less. If you write us a note I'll try to pay attention to it."

84

83 *"Little Beirut," Harlem,*
1988.

84 *"Little Beirut," 1998.*
Three of the buildings have
been demolished, and the
rest are still vacant, except
for two stores and a
storefront church.

85 *Store at the corner of*
132nd Street and Madison
Avenue, 1998.

85

86 *Detail of a building on
131st Street, 1997.*

86

87

Triangle Building, Harlem

Flatiron-style buildings like the Triangle Building on Saint Nicholas Avenue in Harlem line city streets, such as Broadway in Manhattan and Milwaukee Avenue in Chicago, where street intersections form a narrow wedge of land. Structures such as these were designed to link together the various street corners and give urban coherence to the intersection. They fit the spot. Because of the unusual shape of the triangular site, a former manufacturing plant like this one in Harlem would, if demolished, likely be replaced by a park.

The Triangle Building, a former factory, has survived fires and decades of neglect. In its heyday "they had a little bit of everything down there, a hero shop, doctors' offices, cleaners, a recreation center," said a neighbor from across the street in 1998.

The building is now in a program for renovation. Ibo Balton of Housing Preservation and Development says that "the first floor will have commercial development, the second floor will have offices for a church, and the top floors will be lofts."

87 *Triangle Building, Harlem, 1993.*

88

89

88 *Detail of the Triangle Building, 1998.*

89 *Detail of "Country Folks Submarines Home of the Poor Boy Sub" sign on the Triangle Building, 1997.*

90 *A squatter at the entrance to the Triangle Building, 1996.*

Blackstone Building, Gary

The elegant three-story Blackstone Build-ing, located just a few blocks from the U.S. Steel Gary Works plant, absorbed nearly a century of smoke and soot from the gigan-tic mills. Yet the brick and stone structure took the grime and neglect well, like one of those rare faces that acquires nobility and character with age.

I saw two state inspectors posting warn-ing signs saying "Asbestos, a cancer pro-ducing disease." According to a passerby, "It got abandoned. It is a landmark of Gary. Landmarks always get abandoned around here." The owner of the garage across the street said that in the good days "there were parties going on at the same time on all three floors." About the appear-ance of the building, he commented: "One day I was sitting here looking at it and I said to myself that the brickwork must have cost a lot of money, all that in and

out. I don't understand why they say it can-not be fixed; I have seen buildings worse than that put together."

An intoxicated man, who lives in a nearby high-rise for the elderly, said that the building had been a whorehouse for the Gary police. Frank, the last owner of the Blackstone Bar and Grill, had some stories to tell. I found him outside his new place on Virginia Street selecting melons. The only thing he said he misses about his old building is its location. Of the structure itself, he said, "I don't think that is a land-mark. It is a plain old building that needed repairs. There are plenty like that in Gary." He also added: "The Gary police ran it. Blacks were not allowed in the Blackstone twenty-five years ago." For three years Frank paid the eight-hundred-dollar monthly rent to three Gary policemen, later finding out that the building was

owned by the state of Indiana. "They laughed when they took my last check," he said, and continued picking melons.

91 *Detail of the Blackstone Building, 1996.*

92   *Blackstone Building, 1989.*

93   *Blackstone Building, 1993.*

94   *Blackstone Building, 1998.*

95   *Site of the Blackstone Building, 1998.*

The Late Calvin Earle of Eleventh Street, Camden: An American Robinson Crusoe

In the 1930s Calvin Earle came to Camden, where he worked in construction and raised a family in a small house on Eleventh Street. I met him in 1982 as I was documenting a phenomenon common at the time: Calvin's block on Eleventh Street had but one inhabitant, Calvin himself. He stood behind the screen door at the back of his row house while his German shepherd barked at me from the tiny backyard.

Calvin was seventy-eight years old at the time. A trim, neat man, a little stiff in his movements, he was possessed by rage over the fact that his neighborhood had slowly been drained of people and buildings, that it had, in effect, been taken from him. The immediate problem that concerned him was that he shared a wall with an open, abandoned row house, which was used as a dumping site. It was a breeding ground for rats, and the rats came into his house. I arranged for a reporter to interview him, hoping that if his situation were described in the paper, readers moved by it would get him help. Calvin agreed to speak to a reporter.

But when, a few days later, a reporter from the *Philadelphia Inquirer* went to Eleventh Street to do a story along the lines of "An American Robinson Crusoe," Calvin refused to speak to him. He never told me why. I tried to get the board-up program to seal the house next door but was told that, because of the long waiting list and shortage of staff and funds, it could take years before they would get to the house. I persisted, and finally the house

96

97

96 *Calvin Earle's home of thirty years on Eleventh Street in Camden, 1982.*

97 *Calvin Earle's home, 1985.*

98 *Calvin Earle's home, 1998.*

98

was sealed. Calvin was very pleased. Two or three years later the attached house and other vacant units on the block were demolished and Calvin's house was the only structure left on the block.

The image of Calvin gesticulating outside his house is unforgettable: "This used to be all houses around here. You had stores all around. Within five blocks you could buy everything you needed." His arm would sweep in the direction of the overgrown lots where some form of paradise had once existed, and his voice would grow angrier. He wanted to know who had done this to him. He probably died not knowing why his neighborhood had gone away.

99

100

99 *Calvin Earle in his living room, 1984.*

100 *Calvin Earle outside his house, 1982.*

The Ruination of the Camden Free Public Library

The former Camden Free Public Library, a beautiful Carnegie library in a neoclassical style, was built in 1905 at a cost of over one hundred thousand dollars. Vacant since 1987, it is now a damp, roofless ruin. Theresa Gorman, a reference librarian, remembered that on rainy days people on the second floor "had to use an umbrella to go to the rest room." No repairs were made because the library was preparing to move to a new location, the former local headquarters of a utility company, which the company had given to the city. The copper frame that supported the library's glass roof, left unsecured, was stolen. The cost of rebuilding the library in 1993 was estimated at three and a half million dollars. It took six years for the Camden city council to authorize 150 thousand dollars to put a temporary roof on the structure. At the last minute, however, the city business administrator refused to approve the project. No roof was built. Now, sanitation workers rarely pick up garbage in front of the building.

I have visited the former library at least twice a year for a decade. Inscribed on the facade are the foundation date (July 4, 1904), the names Shakespeare and Longfellow (in blocky relief on the pediment), and "Joey-N-Rosa" (spray painted on the columns).

When I visit, I look around and, if there are no signs of activity, I go inside the crumbling structure. I am aware of being observed by area homeowners who fear the dangerous people who lurk there and the fire that they imagine will flare up at any moment. The drug addicts and alcoholics who use the former library as a shooting gallery, a drinking place, and an unofficial shelter also watch my comings and goings.

Inside, wet plaster covers the floors. Some of the built-in bookcases have been burned for fuel. Syringes and empty cans of malt liquor are strewn on the stairs. The second floor has become a huge planter. At the center of what was once a wood-paneled reading room, the light streaming in nourishes several trees. I was amazed by this sight and regarded the trees as symptomatic of the structure's ruination. They grow like any other trees. They have delicate green leaves in early summer and lose them in the winter. They turn yellow in autumn.

Robert Thomson, a city preservation official, has stated that everyone can share the blame for the building's destruction. There is enough to spread around. Four reasons account for its demise: no organized group loudly demanded its restoration; no realistic new use for the building was proposed; the library is far from the Delaware River waterfront, Camden's only area of redevelopment; and, as a "matter of priorities," the impoverished city has more humanitarian needs than saving an old landmark.

I often tell architects and artists about the Camden Free Public Library, explaining that I find nobility in this library, resent the way it has been discarded, and intend to show it respect. Photographing the changing foliage and charting the growth of the trees inside and the decay outside may seem mad or eccentric, but instead I find that I have aroused their interest.

A young architect once asked me for the location of the library, explaining that his client, a wealthy businessman, was looking for a building to house his private library. The latter had been searching for substantial structures in cities like New Haven, where he had purchased a vacant firehouse to store his antique automobile collection. He would not be discouraged by Camden's reputation.

When I spoke to a group of preservationists about the building's plight, an audience member argued that the former library's transformation had gone too far to return it to its original purpose: "Now the building is a biosphere, and it should be preserved as that."

Seeing the photographs, people have reacted as if it were normal for a Carnegie library to be abandoned. They have focused instead on the phenomenon of the trees. A Detroit developer thought that it was "nice"

101

102

to have the trees "protected from the elements." My Puerto Rican friend Carmen, a long-time resident of Camden, is relieved. "The City of Camden has been chopping down trees everywhere," she tells me. She is happy to hear that the abandoned public library on Broadway protects trees. Smiling, she says, "soon the birds will come."

103 *The second-floor reading room, Camden Library, summer 1997.*

104 *The second-floor reading room, Camden Library, winter 1997.*

105 *The second-floor reading room, Camden Library, fall 1998.*

106 *Front stairways, Camden Library, 1999.*

106

Corn Exchange Bank, Harlem

Until 1997, the former Corn Exchange Bank stood out from a distance. It was taller and more massive than anything else on its Harlem block. In this part of Harlem there are few red-brick buildings, and even fewer are as richly decorated. Designed in 1883 as Mount Morris Bank by Lamb and Rich Architects, the building was distinguished by its Romanesque Revival–style base and the eclectic Queen Anne style above its second story. It became the Corn Exchange Bank in 1913 and was declared a landmark of New York in 1993, after standing vacant for more than two decades. There were many plans to rehabilitate the building as a community institution, but because of lack of funding they were never implemented. Then, in 1997, the building lost two floors to a fire. Now, with its first two floors hidden by scaffolding and its top missing, the once beautiful edifice is a grotesque sight.

In the early 1990s I came across a film crew making the movie *Malcolm X* on the corner of 125th Street and Park Avenue. The intersection had been transformed for the filming; they had replaced the street lights and signs, and period cars were parked in front. The bank's main entrance appeared to be in use. Afterward, the entrance was resealed, but a transom window above the door remained as Hollywood's contribution to the building's restoration.

I never slept inside this Harlem building. I never ate a meal there. Still, I have had a personal relationship with it for half of my life. It is near my home. I felt comfortable going there, and I often used the lobby as a setting for portraits and interviews. I thought that in choosing this setting I would not need to explain what I meant by ruins.

It was necessary to squeeze in through a bent metal door and climb a broken stairway to reach the big hall. The ceiling caved in long ago, and a heavy wooden beam used to hang from it, one of its ends touching the floor, the other threatening to fall at any

107

107 *Corn Exchange Bank, Harlem, 1982.*

108 *Corn Exchange Bank, 1992.*

109 *Corn Exchange Bank, 1999.*

108

109

moment. A classical cast-iron column rusted in the middle of the room. An open safe contained political pamphlets left over from the Abraham Beame mayoral campaign—the building had served as its Harlem headquarters. On the floor were strewn a jacket, a rubber boot, a book in Arabic, and several bottles and cups, all covered with a thick coat of plaster and dust. The stairs were cinderblocked, barring access to the French apartments upstairs. Nor could I climb to the roof or look out on 125th Street from one of the small wrought-iron balconies decorated with sunbursts.

111

110   *Detail of the Corn Exchange Bank, 1993.*

111   *Interior detail of the Corn Exchange Bank, 1996.*

The Decline of Two Shacks, Robbins

Adjacent to the Chicago city limits are three of the poorest suburbs in the nation: Harvey, Ford Heights, and Robbins. Places like these are the most likely recipients of the facilities, institutions, and people that nobody wants. Already a large incinerator for burning the city's waste has been built in Robbins, and, as the Chicago Housing Authority seeks to demolish high-rise public housing, these suburbs will become likely places for relocating their residents.

I photographed two neighboring shacks on Hamlin Avenue in Robbins over a period of seven years. Residents living across the street from the shacks, as well as my Chicago audiences, were not loath to comment. One resident observed: "It has been like that for a long time; it looks bad." Another asked me when I was going "to tear them down." Chicago audiences look apprehensive when they see images like those in this series. A member of the audience, appalled to see the dwellings slowly returning to nature, remarked: "They don't have demolition there." And urban planner Charles Hoch commented, "That is really miserable housing."

I spoke to Palma James, the town's business administrator, who told me that Robbins does in fact have a demolition program. She said that the demolition list has "about one hundred homes waiting" and that funds are coming from the county, but that she did not know if these old shacks were on the list.

112

113

114

115

112 *Two shacks in Robbins, 1991.*

113 *Two shacks, 1996.*

114 *Two shacks, 1997.*

115 *Two shacks, 1998.*

South Park Calvary Presbyterian Church, Newark: "The Skin"

The South Park Presbyterian Church made me confront my lack of appreciation for the classical style. Maybe it is because I mistrust banks, the government, and the rich that I find timeless perfection to be exclusionary and cold. Yet even this could not keep me from being impressed by the church's Ionic columns and the warm color of its Nova Scotia brownstone. The structure was designed in 1855 by architect John Welch. Abraham Lincoln delivered a short speech from its front steps. Now, "it does not have a very bright future. We're going to be very lucky if we can just get someone to fix the facade," says Elizabeth Del Tufo, a Newark preservationist.

I first entered the church in 1987, when it was a homeless shelter. The sign on the door read "Free Lunch, South Park Light House Temple 12–2 P.M., Backdoor." The day I walked in, the caterers were devotees of Hare Krishna, and people were lined up to receive a brown vegetarian dish with stale doughnut accompaniments.

In an extension of the church's interior, a lone nurse was dealing as best she could with clients with frozen toes, broken limbs, chronic colds, AIDS, and tuberculosis, people who suffered from malnutrition and, quite often, substance abuse. Their ashen skin and lips suggested that they often slept in the street, exposed to the elements, and occasionally sought shelter in abandoned buildings.

Soon after my visit, the city of Newark declared the building unsafe, and the homeless shelter moved to a nearby garage. The church burned to the ground, leaving its landmark facade standing. The architect David Abrahmson calls this "the Skin." Water has been filtering through the ruin and threatens it with collapse. One architect has estimated that it would cost about 250 thousand dollars just to stabilize the facade.

Troy West, a professor of architecture at the New Jersey Institute of Technology, envisions attaching a new glass structure to the back of the facade as a stop for a light-

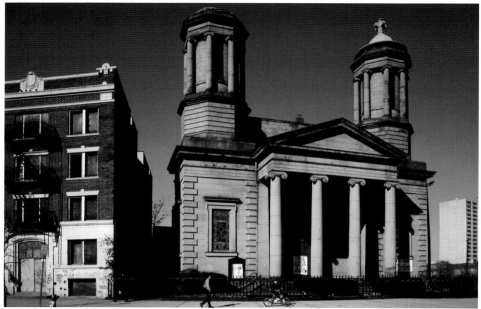

116

117

rail system. That light rail, however, might never be built, and, if it is, it is likely to travel in the opposite direction. Vicky Snoy of Prudential Insurance would like to see a garden planted behind the facade.

What remains of the former South Park Presbyterian Church is on the northeast corner of Lincoln Park, an area that at the turn of the century housed the city's upper

class. Now the large mansions have become live-in drug rehabilitation centers. Integrity House, one of these institutions, regularly cleans the graffiti from the church and maintains flowers on the steps where Lincoln once spoke.

118

116 *South Park Calvary Presbyterian Church, Newark, 1989.*

117 *South Park Presbyterian Church, 1998.*

118 *South Park Presbyterian Church, 1996.*

119 *South Park Presbyterian Church after a fire, 1997. Only the facade stands.*

119

120

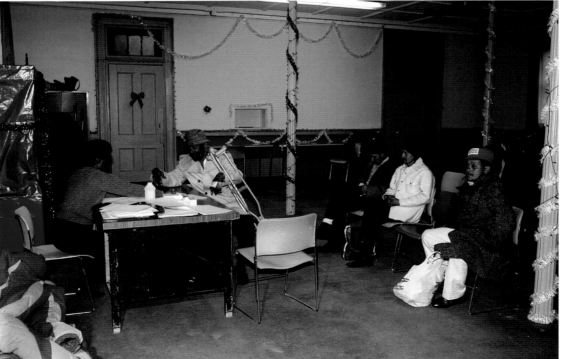

121

120 *South Park Presbyterian Church, 1987. The church became South Park Light House Temple, which housed a soup kitchen and homeless shelter run by the temple until the building was declared unsafe.*

121 *South Park Presbyterian Church, 1987. A visiting nurse examines her homeless patients in South Light House Temple.*

City Methodist Church, Gary

122

122 *City Methodist Church, Gary, 1998.*

What was the point of its time-defying design if the City Methodist Church was to last only a half century? Why was so much steel and Indiana Bedford limestone invested in it? The Gothic Revival structure was built in 1925, at a cost twenty times greater than that of the structure it replaced. Half of the cost was donated by U.S. Steel, and Judge Elbert Gary, city founder and president of U.S. Steel, donated its spectacular organ.

According to Gary historian James Lane, the church was built by Reverend William Grant Seaman, who envisioned it and its facilities serving as a magnet to bring people together. "There in the heart of a rushing, bustling city, there amid the greedy, grasping throng, it shall...hold its quiet arms to the weary and the oppressed," wrote Tom Cannon in a 1926 poem, "Dreams of the Twilight—The City Church," which celebrated the church's inauguration. Reverend Seaman was ahead of his time, often inviting black choirs to sing in the church. But the congregation objected to his multi-racial vision and fired him. John Laui, a high school teacher who grew up in Gary, described the church: "My father went there. It was not only a church, it was a real center of social activity. As children, we took the bus from there to go to Wrigley Field and Kaminski Park in Chicago."

After it ceased functioning as a church, City Methodist housed Indiana University Northwest and later a dance school. Vacant for about two decades, it has been vulnerable to theft. Its copper gutters and some of its stone facing have been stolen. It is now overgrown with trees. Its choir has collapsed; its

123

floor boards have broken. Several of the windows have been removed, and it has suffered a major fire.

To some members of the congregation, City Methodist seemed too ornate, even popish. Now the ornamentation consists of holes, broken windows, liquor bottles, pigeons, dead squirrels, and vegetation. In the afternoon, warm light filters into the high vaulted nave through amber-toned stained-glass windows. People do not congregate here anymore, and the columns, arches, and broken floorboards are covered with dust and droppings. Instead of human voices and the harmonies of the manual Aeolian-Skinner organ, the fluttering of wings and the cooing of pigeons fills the air.

Outside I met Gilbert, the maintenance man for the senior citizens high-rise next door. "People want the church destroyed," he told me. He himself preferred building a parking lot. I mentioned that Gary already seems more like a parking lot than a city, that there is no need for more parking space, but it made no impression on him.

123 *Interior of the City Methodist Church, 1998.*

124 *Interior of the City Methodist Church, 1998.*

125 *Interior of the City Methodist Church, 1998.*

124

125

Northeastern High School, Detroit: A Different Era of Public Architecture

126

Northeastern High School was a fine steel-frame building, made of dark brown brick. It faced a city park. The style of the school combined Beaux-Arts grandeur with the functional design of factories, coupling a feeling of order with intimidating elegance. For Gary Sands, a professor of urban planning, the edifice was a reminder of a different era of public architecture.

The area around the school once had the richest property-tax base of all the city's high school districts. There were so many factories and properties that generated tax revenues there that part of the wealth was distributed to poorer districts around the city. Most of the local Polish, Ukrainian, and German immigrants who lived in the area worked in the automobile plants nearby, and women worked in the many cigar factories.

Artists have been fascinated by this ruined school. On two of the school's cinderblocked entrances, artist Tyree Guyton drew crude but vital images of a man and a woman, which I call the "Adam and Eve of Detroit." Their simple straight lines complement the building, and the primitive style and subject of the composition suggest a passage backward in time. Later Guyton added an icon of his grandfather, Sam, on the other cinderblocked entrance. Nancy Patek, a painter, was planning to do an oil painting of the ruined school, but, before she had a chance to begin, the bulldozers had demolished it. As she told *Detroit News*, "On the one hand, I am delighted with the rebirth of the city but depressed because I'm running out of new material to paint."

126 *Northeastern High School,
East Side of Detroit, 1995.*

127 *Northeastern High School,
1998.*

Union Station, Gary

In May 1998, the Great American Station Foundation of Washington, D.C., included Gary's Union Station on its list of the top ten endangered historic train stations. This was the description:

> Gary Union Station is one of the best surviving examples of famed Chicago architect and planner Daniel Burnham. It is an excellent example of beaux-arts design applied to station architecture. Throughout America, there are few other stations of this period and design still remaining, and in the Calumet region of Indiana, Gary Union Station is one of the last great monuments of the golden age of both railroading and steel making. Built in 1910 to serve passengers of the New York Central System and the Baltimore and Ohio Railroad, the once grand and elegant and now threatened station has been vacant for many years.

I was excited to read in the description that Union Station was by Burnham, the architect of Chicago's Field Museum and Grant Park whose motto was "Make no little plans." But it turns out that the press release was incorrect. The station was designed by R. A. Lang, a company architect for the Baltimore and Ohio Railroad.

The Twentieth Century Limited stopped at Union Station on its way to New York. The Capitol Limited stopped there on its way to Washington, D.C. The city of Gary purchased the edifice in 1994 from the executors of the former Penn Central Corporation for a mere fifteen thousand dollars. There have been discussions about turning the old depot into a steel museum, a railroad museum, or both, but the building is cut off from the city by Interstate 90, and there is no real community support for it.

The city allowed Fred Williamson, a native son and former professional football player turned actor and producer, to shoot scenes for the 1995 movie *Original Gangstas* inside the building. Because of its isolation from the city, the old depot was the ideal gangsta hangout. According to Christopher Meyers, a former preservation officer for Gary, the station had been mothballed, but the movie makers "removed the plywood from the openings, broke the floorboards, and gutted a lot of the building for their own use." Once a very popular building, Union Station is one of Gary's rare landmarks. Its future looks bleak.

129

130

128 *Union Station, Gary, 1998.*

129 *Interior of Union Station, 1998.*

130 *Celebrating the former Union Station on a wall at Gateway Park, 1998.*

Bushwick Theater, Brooklyn: "Let the Good Times Roll"

131

132

Brooklyn's Broadway is a long commercial street with many stores that were set on fire during the blackout of 1977. It remains one of the nation's most devastated streets. The Bushwick Theater, a once elegant triangular structure, stands covered in scaffolding at the Monroe Street intersection. It has already lost its marquee and its balusters, and the scaffolding protects passersby from falling debris. The theater's days are numbered.

Even today, however, the Beaux-Arts facade of the Bushwick Theater promises fun. Oversize baroque putti, with chubby cheeks and joyful smiles, flank medallions above the windows. Smaller putti blowing trumpets hover above the entrances, and sculpted heads bearing dramatic expressions epitomize the idea of the theatrical. The cornice is richly ornamented with terra-cotta wreaths.

133

The theater, with three balconies inside, once accommodated thousands of people. It was a major stop on the vaudeville circuit, hosting Ethel Barrymore and other headliners like Mae West, Eddie Cantor, and Jack Benny. Its last tenant was the Pilgrim Baptist Cathedral, which moved into the building in 1970 and moved out in the early 1980s. The building is for sale, but nobody seems to be interested. Community Board Number 3 has said that nothing concerning the building has passed through its hands, and that nobody wants to demolish, reuse, or remodel it.

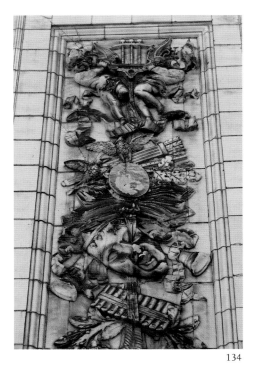

134

131 *Bushwick Theater, Brooklyn, 1989.*

132 *Detail of the Bushwick Theater, 1997.*

133 *Bushwick Theater, 1999.*

134 *Detail of the Bushwick Theater, 1999.*

135

Riviera Theater, Detroit: A "Pretty Playhouse"

136

The Riviera Theater, one of Detroit's great neighborhood movie houses, used to take up the northeast corner of Riviera Street and Grand River Boulevard. It was built in 1926 by John Eberson, an architect famous for his fantastic "picture palaces." Designed in a hybrid Italian Renaissance style of yellow brick with terra-cotta ornament, the Riviera was one of Eberson's grandest structures. Griffins supporting escutcheons appeared around the top of the theater's hexagonal tower.

One late afternoon in 1996, I set off on my usual visit to the theater only to find that the building was being demolished by a drunk operating a decrepit yellow crane. By this time only half the building was left, but I could still see the crimson velvet curtains on the stage. Approaching them, I

137

was stopped by the crane operator, waving
his arms.

In 1997 I stood on the same spot where
I used to photograph the Riviera, but this
time I photographed clouds. A man coming out of a bank asked me what I was
doing, and I told him I was photographing
the Riviera Theater. When he looked at
me in surprise, I asked him if he saw it. He
told me that he had seen the Riviera on
that corner for more than twenty years,
and that for him the building would always
be there.

On my latest visit to the corner, in September 1998, I found that the decrepit yellow crane with all its markings erased had
been discarded on the site of its last job. It
just stood there rusting on the vacant lot.

138

135 *Riviera Theater, Detroit, 1993.*

136 *Stage, Riviera Theater, 1996.*

137 *Riviera Theater, 1996.*

138 *Site of the Riviera Theater, 1997.*

Clinton Avenue Trust, Newark: Now New Jersey's Largest Funerary Monument

139

When I first encountered the former Clinton Avenue Trust, at the corner of Clinton Avenue and Chadwick Street, it presided over one of Newark's most active drug centers. In 1980 it housed the Inner City University and later became a flea market until it was abandoned in the late 1880s.

Until the mid-1990s, the intersection was a favorite place for teenagers to "do the doughnut": a form of circus in which late-model cars, just stolen, were driven in circles as fast as possible. The show would begin with people standing in an improvised ring, waiting. The car would then come up the hill at full speed, its engine roaring at maximum acceleration, and the driver would clamp on the brakes. Tires would screech and burn in a cloud of rising black smoke. The shiny vehicles were destroyed in seconds. The drivers were often very young

and inexperienced, and the police would not pursue them for fear of causing an accident. A man named Hassan reminisced about the drivers' skill: "Them kids be thirteen, fourteen years old, and they shift gears in the four corners. You have to make sure you don't touch the corner. You don't find race drivers doing that." The excited crowd feared being run over by an out-of-control vehicle. There was something exhilarating about seeing the beautiful cars with their powerful engines screeching and roaring. It was the closest thing to a bullfight I have ever seen in the United States.

I did not expect the Clinton Trust to become a funerary monument, however. When Hakim, alias "One Shot," was killed in front of it in 1996, Mack, a homeless man who lived inside the vacant building, painted a memorial landscape and a por-

trait of his friend. According to the teenagers who still hang out at the corner, the police destroyed One Shot's portrait because it glorified the gangsta lifestyle.

When Darnett Daniels, a.k.a. "Strawberry," was shot and killed, a small memorial of plastic flowers and a stuffed bear was placed in her memory at the old bank's main entrance. In sixty years the Clinton Trust has gone from being a temple to the accumulation of capital to an improvised and temporary memorial to the casualties of inner-city violence.

140

141

139 *Clinton Avenue Trust, Newark, 1998.*

140 *Detail of Clinton Trust: memorial to "Strawberry," 1998.*

141 *Detail of Clinton Trust: a funereal landscape mural dedicated to the memory of "One Shot," 1998.*

Tufts Fireproof Warehouse, Chicago

Number 4444 West Madison Street was a storage warehouse typical of those built in Chicago in the 1920s. As people began to move from houses to apartments, or inherited valuables from relatives, they needed a place to store their excess belongings. These establishments, located all over the city, provided secure storage for furniture, pianos, china, and the like. To convey a sense of safety and solidity, the warehouses had richly detailed facades and comfortable ground-floor offices.

Soon after being abandoned, the Tufts Fireproof Warehouse lost most of its ornamentation. In 1998 I could not find the structure on West Madison Street. Most of the block was gone. It was as if the warehouse had never existed—"like a blip on a TV screen," in the words of local historian Tim Samuelson. The owner of a nearby resale shop looked at my photograph of the building and, indicating an empty lot to the west, said: "It was right there." Guided by a garage that had appeared in the background of an earlier photo and by a street light to the west of the building, I found the spot and took a picture of the empty space the warehouse had once occupied. A motorcycle raced by in front of my camera, and, in an instant, it too had disappeared.

142

143

144

142 *Tufts Fireproof Warehouse,
West Side of Chicago, 1987.*

143 *Tufts Fireproof Warehouse,
1997.*

144 *Site of the Tufts Fireproof
Warehouse, 1998.*

145

Section of East Forty-Seventh Street, Chicago: Home of the Blues

Three solid buildings once stood together on the north side of East Forty-seventh Street, east of Martin Luther King Boulevard, the remnants of an African-American business community that reached its height in the 1920s. One, the Henderson Funeral Home, was built in 1929, its facade decorated with green Art Deco terra-cotta tiles modeled by artists who had been brought from France by a Chicago terra-cotta manufacturer. The elegant edifice was originally an African-American funeral association where people could make advance payments on their own send-offs. To the right was another Art Deco terra-cotta building originally occupied by a furniture store, its big windows giving passersby a good view of all three stories of merchandise within.

The third, a modest two-story structure, most recently housed a business that bought and sold jewelry, used items, and beepers and also had a taxi service. The buildings were demolished in 1997.

In the 1920s boom the street boasted stores and offices by day and theaters and nightclubs by night, featuring some of the most famous black show-business personalities of the period. After the depression of 1929 diminished its economic steam, the street became home to taverns that catered to new arrivals from the Mississippi Delta with live blues performances by such legends as Muddy Waters and Howlin' Wolf. Today, across the street stands a large empty lot with a sign that announces a projected Museum of the Blues.

146

147

The painted window seals on the former furniture store were a delight. They were playful black-and-white designs done in a style reminiscent of Edward Gorey's, suggesting in each window the goings-on in a whorehouse: a man in a top hat—a flaneur, I thought—looked intently out a window; others wore heavy coats as if they had just come in or were ready to leave. Each of the top story's windows had large painted curtains arranged differently, giving the scenes a theatrical feel. A naked woman, shown from the back, sat at a table with a man. On the ground floor loud paintings of blues performers labeled "Legends" contrasted with the fading black-and-white scenes above. Now all that is left of these three buildings is an empty lot, but a few fragments were spared.

Father Donald Rowe, a Jesuit priest with an interest in architectural artifacts, salvaged some of the terra-cotta pieces from the funeral home and integrated them into a wall at the Saint Ignatius Preparatory School in Chicago. He wanted the students to enjoy their beauty and called them "part of Chicago history—in an age of disposable plastic objects—very beautiful objects, good for the children to experience." He added that "the purpose is education. The artifacts will make the children more interested in the history of their city. Their lives will be richer."

148 *Terra-cotta ornament from the Henderson Funeral Home on the walls of the Saint Ignatius Preparatory School, Chicago, 1998.*

Essex County Jail, Newark

149

149 *Essex County Jail, Central Ward of Newark, December 1998.*

A man walking by the former jail once told me that this overgrown ruin might become the site of a new magnet high school or perhaps a new biotech company. He said that the old prison is structurally safe but not socially safe—that homeless people lived there. He added that if I were to go in with at least two other people, however, I would be safe.

In the 1970s I had read reports that overcrowding at the Essex County Jail was made unbearable by summer heat and humidity. Now empty of prisoners, encircled by tall, ivy-covered stone—like an English ruin—the former jail looks pleasant. The jail is the oldest government building in Newark. It was built in 1837 by John Haviland, the prison architect made famous for designing New York City's notorious "Tombs" and Philadelphia's Eastern State

Penitentiary. Like many mid-nineteenth-century prisons, its design included underground dungeons, where men were shackled to the walls, fed bread and water, and shut off from the light of day. Most of Essex County's hangings took place there. Its execution chamber was active until 1902 when local hangings were superseded by electrocutions held at the state prison. The building was greatly expanded and remodeled in 1890 and again in 1907. The Essex County Jail is about paying for one's crimes. Its horrors, like those of its big sister, the Eastern State Penitentiary, must have driven people to insanity.

Certain odors inside the hulking ruin are pervasive: rusted iron, wet plaster, and decomposing paper. Rusting bars are everywhere: to the left, to the right, and above. There is little space to move about; even

150

150 *View along second-floor hallway of the Essex County Jail, 1998.*

being free in this jail feels like imprisonment. I imagine the screaming, the clanking of metal, the swearing, crying, and praying that went on inside, but I can't imagine how it all blended together. What were the sounds of this place?

In four wings there are a total of four hundred tiny cells arranged in tiers on three, sometimes on four, floors. Most of the toilets and sinks have been removed. When I first visited, I found a cell decorated with women's high-heeled shoes and graffiti left by a film crew. Nearby, a dog barked. I became aware of being alone, and I left.

A month later, I returned with four friends, and this time we visited all the wings, the heating plant, and the laundry room. I entered a room full of what looked like video games and later learned that they were slot machines confiscated from illegal gambling operations. In my search for the solitary-confinement cells, I could not find

an entrance to the basement. Throughout the cells, offices, and bathrooms, we discovered drug paraphernalia carefully arranged on top of chairs, tables, and toilets with planks on top of them.

The jail was closed in the early 1970s because there were too many breakouts. Then the county's Bureau of Narcotics Control used the building for offices until it was declared structurally unsafe in 1989. The building was a convenient place for questioning tipsters who did not want to be seen. The cells served both as holding pens for some of the informants and as places to keep records.

One of the cells was covered with bound notebooks, each containing thousands of legal records. The books, almost a century old, contained detailed handwritten records of people's mortgages. The narcotics bureau left behind more documents. I found them strewn along a hallway. In cells, I found stacks of arrest

records containing names, addresses, mug shots, and fingerprints, some dating from as recently as 1980. Included were the names of the arresting officers, a description of the arrest, and the names of the perpetrator's close relatives. In a folder of the county's criminal investigation records, found inside a cell, was the entry "Scars, Marks, and Amps" containing the following descriptions: "Howie, Scar under right eye, 3–4 scars on the forehead and pock marks under the right eye"; "Amir, 2 inch scar on right leg"; "Francisco, Tattoo on left side of chest"; "Albert, old needle scars inside of both forearms." Another room contained records of wiretaps.

At first I weighed the desire to inform the public about the arrest files against my need to continue documenting the jail. I called a friend at the *New York Times* and suggested a story, aware that this would change the site and possibly prompt the authorities to remove the documents and seal the building. I was afraid that my action would somehow erase the horror of the place.

On my third visit, I was accompanied by David Herszenhorn, a Newark reporter, and the photographer Norman Lone. We met historians Kenneth T. Jackson and Clement Price at the jail. Jackson's first concern was with the building's preservation. Remarking that New Jersey had no prison museum, Jackson asked if executions had taken place there, because that would make the jail a more attractive candidate for a museum. Price wondered if the folders on the floor contained the arrest records from the Newark riots. He was excited and said that he would bring his history of Newark class to visit the site. The next week Herszenhorn told me that the Essex County Jail had indeed been the main holding place for people during the 1967 riots.

151 *Interior of the Essex County Jail, 1998.*

152

153

Little realizes that he does not know his real name and adopts the surname X. He learns that he is "in that wilderness called North America."

In his research, Herszenhorn phoned the mother of a former inmate, the father of seven children, who had died of AIDS. She told him that "he went to prison to pay for what he did." He also reached a woman who refused to believe he had her arrest file (for possession of narcotics and welfare fraud) until he read her mother's name and date of birth from the file. The woman, who now has a job and had been able to remake her life after leaving prison, was appalled to learn that her records and picture were available to anyone. As she said, "It could have gotten into the wrong hands and done damage to a lot of people."

At present, a federally supported 350-million-dollar Science Park is planned for the fourteen-acre site, which includes the jail. Since the building is on the National Register of Historic Places, a feasibility study for its reuse was made. The five-hundred-page study stated that because the cell walls are bearing walls, the structure cannot be gutted without the roof collapsing. It also suggested using it as a generating plant for the science park.

I envision with dismay a sanitized prison. Preservationists may want to restore the jail instead of transforming it into a generating plant. There would be many decrees. Sweep up the records and the floors; rebuild the roof and reinforce the foundations; replace the iron bars and doors; add many new coats of paint; cut all the weeds (including those tall green plants with giant leaves by the laundry that so puzzled us); remove all the tires and car parts dumped there illegally; in short, make the prison as clean as a Marriott Hotel, as Ellis Island, as Grand Central Station, and build a restaurant and a souvenir shop on the grounds.

We preserve the past by freezing it in time, taming it. This is our way of rendering incomprehensible this "wilderness called North America."

I later saw a headline from a 1992 article in the *Star Ledger:* "Astute film viewers will recognize scenes from New Jersey in one of the most talked about films of the day." The prison scenes in *Malcolm X* were filmed there in late 1991. When I saw the movie again I realized that director Spike Lee took several liberties with the building. He shot exteriors in different buildings, varied the size and shape of the cells to suit his needs. In one of these scenes, Malcolm

154

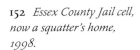

152 *Essex County Jail cell, now a squatter's home, 1998.*

153 *Essex County Jail cell, 1998. Exceptionally, the sink and toilet are still in place.*

154 *Iron bars and tiny cells in the Essex County Jail, 1998.*

155 *Office floor of the Essex County Jail, 1998. Rotting arrest records include a file labeled "Exhibit A" and another labeled "done."*

155

Woodland Cemetery, Newark

156

Woodland Cemetery, also known as the German Cemetery, served the white population of Newark's Central Ward until the 1950s. After that population moved to the suburbs, the cemetery offered the area's lowest-priced burials, and its clients became those on public assistance. Destitute people were buried here in twenty-five-by-thirty-five-foot trenches. Woodland remained active until the early 1980s, when it ran out of space. Lacking funds and security staff, it has fallen prey to vandalism and illegal dumping. Its desolate landscape has served as an ideal place for doing drugs. It is also a site for local voodoo cults.

The management tried various approaches in their struggle to keep the cemetery from further decaying and to curtail vandalism and dumping. To enlist the support of veterans organizations, they showed that there were hundreds of veterans' graves among the sixty thousand people buried in the cemetery. They emphasized, too, that Woodland had not been a segregated cemetery and asked the community to keep an eye on the grounds and help keep them clean. Finally, management appealed

to the general public by searching for the graves of famous people. All they turned up was the grave of Steven Brody, the sole person known to have survived a jump from the Brooklyn Bridge. None of this worked very well.

The cemetery's Gothic Revival gate, referred to as "the lodge," is a surprisingly small brownstone structure topped with an elegant iron cross, something out of a medieval German village. Flowers and bushes, once brought to decorate graves, are now incorporated into the vegetation. Rich plantings spread wildly everywhere. The grounds sloping down toward the east and the vegetation covering the stones give the overall impression of a peaceful wildlife refuge.

157

156 *German Gothic Revival entrance to Woodland Cemetery, Central Ward of Newark, 1988.*

157 *Angel with broken wings: "In memory of William I. Book,* born 1844, died 1911," Woodland Cemetery, 1993.

158 *Woodland Cemetery, 1988.*

159 *Woodland Cemetery, 1993.*

158

159

CHAPTER THREE

Assorted Broken and Wasted Things

Arena que la vida se llevo.
(Sand being carried away by time.)
　　—From a tango by Homero Manzi

HEBREW INSTITUTE OF UNIVERSITY HEIGHTS

160

160 *Section of the Hebrew Institute of University Heights (closed for more than fifteen years), South Bronx, 1987.*

Ageless No More: A Crushed, Cast-Off Mickey Mouse

Mickey Mouse is very popular in the ghettos of the United States. He is a life force, always on the move. The feisty cartoon character is pervasive throughout the culture. In Gary I was stopped by the sight of this eyeless, toothless Mickey lying in an alley. Edward Perry, a local resident, shared my curiosity and responded: "A dead Mickey Mouse; that is unusual. You usually keep a Mickey Mouse all your life. It still has good ears. They ought to give it to the Good Will so that they can put it back together and give it to another kid." Perry went on to explain parenthetically, "Mickey does not represent one race. Walt Disney designed them so that they could be everybody. He understood the color of money."

161

161 *Discarded Mickey Mouse in an alley, Gary, 1997.*

162 *Shy, a dead pit bull left in an alley in Watts, Los Angeles, 1996.*

163 *Dead pit bull, South Central Los Angeles, 1997. A Latino woman walking by with her two children covered their eyes and took a detour to avoid it.*

Animals

Often, in poor areas of cities, when people die or move away, they leave their dogs behind. Others, finding the cost of pet food prohibitive, are forced to get rid of their pets. Alfredo, a worker in a seed store that sells dog food in South Central Los Angeles, says that "people abandon sick dogs. They throw them out of the house." It is common to find sick and hungry animals roaming the streets, foraging for food or seeking refuge in derelict buildings. Some die inside ruins; others get run over by cars and are left lying on the sidewalk.

Clandestine dog fights are common in Los Angeles. While driving along the alleys of the city, I frequently encountered dead pit bulls left inside garbage bags, rolled in old carpets, or simply left exposed, to rot.

In the late 1980s, a group called "Alley Animals of Baltimore" convinced the director of housing for the city to place a warning on the boards in case animals were trapped inside sealed buildings: "PRIVATE PROPERTY/NO TRESPASSING/ NO LOITERING/IF ANIMAL TRAPPED

PLEASE CALL 410 396 6286." I called the local number given on the warning and was told that "cats can get in through a small space and then forget how they got in." If someone calls with a complaint the department tries to send someone to release the animal.

164

164 *Bones of a dog on a fire escape, South Bronx, 1990. Anthropologist Drew Walker said, "The bones were left there and all the rest trickled down the fire escape. You could have seen how he lay there. He died in the summer and probably had a fever; if it had been cool, he would have gone inside to die. The fire escape was a nice place to die—pretty comfortable, no ticks or bugs."*

Neon Signs: "Blinkety Blinkers"

165

165 *Neon signs advertising appliances on West Madison Street, West Side of Chicago, 1992.*

At night, when much of the urban texture lies hidden in darkness, neon signs tell the story of "what the place is," according to preservationist Garrick Landsberg. Philip Hazard, an artist who has worked with neon since 1975, observes: "Neon signs give out an unusual light, a magical energy. Their appeal transcends their function. Neon signs can transform a space. In the rain, reflected on the streets, their colors are beautiful. That is why Hollywood likes them." Neon signs "have a nostalgia appeal—they're a retro thing giving a flavor to a period," explains John Bigger, a Detroit architect. Antique shops fix and sell these old signs. Customers prefer the small ones, like those for a shoe repair shop that once hung in a store window. People take them home and hang them on the walls of their dens. Those made of metal, with the neon tubes encased in porcelain enamel, are called "classics." Their deep blues and reds recall the 1950s.

Sometimes signs are taken from one building and affixed to another. In Los Angeles, architect John Kaliski recently gave me a tour of once-abandoned signs that the city had refurbished, a sure indication of their regained status. But, as Bigger explained, neon signs are impractical for many business: "They're expensive, all that bending of tubes; they're very fragile, they don't hold up very well, and they need pretty high maintenance. They leak gas through the metal connections and are very susceptible to weather changes. People don't want to pay for their upkeep. Money is the bottom line."

166

Hearing people talk about the cost of maintaining and repairing working signs reminds me of signs that are derelict, with fading color and letters and extinguished light bulbs and neon tubes, their rusting metal frames weighing heavily above sidewalks. No longer able to rotate, to change color, or to blink on and off, they are now reminders of the long-gone businesses that used to line the old "streets of lights." These are the signs that are too big to take home: "Nobody is going to bother to repair the rocket ship on the Oldsmobile dealerships," says Chicago historian Tim Samuelson. Usually these derelict signs are taken down and dismantled when they appear in danger of falling.

Along desolate streets, creaking under the blowing wind, extinguished neon signs still add to the urban night's threatening shadows. On a rainy night I prefer those that blink.

166 *"Classic" neon signs on Washington Street, downtown Newark, 1981.*

167 *Extinguished liquor store sign in Harlem, 1998.*

168

169

168 *Sign at an old gas station, West Side of Chicago, 1991. A driver, upon seeing me photograph the sign, said, "It was nice. It may have been worth something."*

169 *Neon sign with later addition, east Detroit, 1998.*

170 *"American Graffiti," Gary, 1998. The name "Jane" is superimposed on the name of the previous store owner.*

171 *Broken, discolored, and rusted sign, Gary, 1998. Visible inside are some of the rocks that broke it.*

170

171

Vehicles of Desire

172

As I traveled through the country's alleys, peering into backyards, the old broken-down cars most often stopped me. I once saw a Buick, parked in the middle of the backyard of a man named Tomas, its front end smashed, its flat tires waiting to be fixed or sold for junk. Yet Tomas did not feel a sense of urgency to do anything. In another backyard, where two years before cars had shared the area with chicken coops and rabbit cages, the automobile had won out. Tool boxes and plastic oil jars now replaced the chickens and the rabbits. Older cars get pushed farther and farther back toward the alley to make room at the front for those that still run. Cars, after years of immobility, would eventually sink into the ground.

Paula Cruz Raiz, who came to South Central Los Angeles from an Indian community in Mazatlan, Mexico, keeps her small chicken coop on the hood of a stripped-down car and ties her guard dog to what remains of its front bumper. Throughout the city the backs of pickup trucks and boats are used to store cans and other recyclables. Not all is lost; potted plants can be grown or birds and even animals raised on the roof of a car. And the car can be used as an extension of the house. One morning I saw a woman in Watts open the back door of a 1948 Cadillac to get a man's suit out of her "car-closet." Sometimes, homeless people rent a place in a car to sleep.

Peter, the owner of a car lot, told me: "The climate in California is dry, and the temperature is mild. Cars don't rust so fast. No need to put all that salt on the roads—in the East cars get eaten up by the salt.

172 *Corvette mural, Detroit, 1997.*

173 *A 1954 Ford, South Central Los Angeles, 1997. The car has been parked in the same spot for fourteen years.*

174 *Chrysler parked in a vacant lot, South Central Los Angeles, 1997.*

173

People want to buy California cars. They're solid." Low riders buy the biggest of the old cars to fix them for show. Then there are those who like the classics, the 1930s and 1940s models made popular by gangster movies, the same cars beloved by the older generation of Mexican-Americans.

A car offered for sale on Crenshaw Boulevard in South Central Los Angeles listed its features on a sign:

1951 BUICK SPECIAL
Four doors. runs good
1988 Oldsmobile Engine
   "   "   Transmission
   "   "   Steering Column
1987 Pontiac Rear End
Power Steering by Jaguar
Power Brakes by Chevy
Electric Trunk Opener
Stereo System—Nice
2 Electric Fuel Pumps (Front & Rear)
1973 Cadillac Electric Seats
   "   "   Sun Visor
Completely New Wiring
Heater—Works Great!!

Latinos tend to be different. According to José, the manager of a tire shop, "They like old things. They don't want to get rid of them just because they don't run. One has a little car; one does not want to throw

174

it away." Besides, Latinos think that they may one day fix the car and sell it at great profit." Javier, a *paletero* (ice cream vendor), said: "It is an old car, but if you paint it and put a new motor in it, it may be worth more than a new one."

Many Los Angeles backyards have been taken over by old, disabled cars. For those who knew the neighborhood when backyards were grassy lawns, this signals deterioration, but the car owners regard the

backyard vehicles with nostalgia. Not only are they reminders of happy times, but there is the ever-present hope of one day fixing them up and selling them for a lot of money.

175

176

177

175 *The rusted skeleton of a luxury car, possibly a 1948 Lincoln, left on a lot at Inland Steel, northwest Indiana, 1980.*

176 *Cars in the South Bronx, 1978.*

177 *Pleasure boat built in the late 1940s, Camden, 1999. Stewart, a cabinet maker, purchased it for five hundred dollars from a lawyer. "Kids got inside and broke everything," he said. The boat, Hernando's Hideaway, has two good engines, but its frame is in disrepair. Despite its derelict appearance, Stewart likes the way it looks standing in his lot.*

178 *Discarded plane, South Central Los Angeles, 1998.*

178

Ordinary Door and Window Seals

179

Seals are intended to protect vacant buildings from fire, vandalism, and the elements. They are made of plywood, brick, cinderblock, or metal and are often left unpainted, but with time, plywood turns from brown to gray and metal rusts. The seals covering the lower floors of a building are often painted gray or dark shades of blue or ochre, colors least likely to call attention to the building's degraded condition. Also, the lower stories of a structure are sealed with a more permanent material such as cinderblock, while plywood or sheet metal is used for the higher floors. The uppermost floors are frequently left unsealed.

Scavengers remove seals to allow light in, and the openings indicate the progress of their work. Squatters often replace the boards with transparent plastic, also to let in light.

Some seals, such as plywood and sheet metal, are easy to pry open with the help of a crowbar or a kick. To make them more secure, contractors screw them to the window frame. Cinderblocks provide a better deterrent because they take time to shatter and vandals do not want to be seen trespassing. Bricks make the best seal because they are more solid and it takes longer to break through them, but they are the most expensive. All coverings must keep out the rain, but they must also permit the sealed building to breathe, lest the inside structure rot. A small corner is cut at the bottom of the boards to let in air.

Recently, a new high-tech metal seal has been introduced in Chicago by an English company. The seals are sturdier and can be rented; the company owns and maintains them. Still, the manager of a

company on the South Side of Chicago who uses these expensive seals could not altogether prevent losses. He has thought of reverting to plywood.

Contractors seek to outbid each other for the contract to board up a building. They track down local disasters by listening to fire scanners, which receive transmissions from fire departments. Even before the flames have subsided, they are seeking out the building owner to negotiate the job. If the owner is not there, or if the building is city-owned, they follow the next fire. Companies with names like Advance, Ace, Active or Aactive vie for the first listing in the Yellow Pages.

Seals cannot protect a building from deterioration over time. Without periodic maintenance, even well-built structures fall apart. Historian Tim Samuelson described

the likely fate of a boarded building in Harlem: "Looks like that whole corner is cracking off. It's ready to fall into the street; that's the death rattle of that building. Moisture gets into those cracks, then freezes in the winter. If [the architectural ornaments] don't break into pieces on the sidewalk, they'll end up in the salvage shop.

"You may work against the neighborhood to keep these buildings as a boarded-up presence, but if you take away the buildings what have you got?" Samuelson asks rhetorically. Sealing is perceived as a "depressing activity," but it is something "better than leaving the building open or an empty lot." Seals have been called "band-aids without any healing power," and politicians rarely boast about them.

One exception was the installation of a new roof and the cinderblocking of the

179 *Facade of the Wilshire, Detroit, 1998. The derelict apartment building once resembled an elegant turn-of-the-century Mediterranean resort.*

180 *Section of a sealed building, South Side of Chicago, 1998. The medieval-revival-style building is in a neighborhood with many drug addicts.*

windows and doors at the former Bronx Borough Courthouse in the South Bronx (see chapter 1). The project cost more than three hundred thousand dollars. More than ten years later, a sign on the facade commemorating the occasion was still visible: "Federal Community Development Program Seal Up Of The Former Night Court, The City Of New York, Edward I. Koch Mayor." It lists six other politicians with their titles.

In the late 1980s, in North Newark, a sign on a boarded window of a substantial corner edifice asked, "Any ideas for this building?" and gave a telephone number to call. The structure is still vacant.

181 *Detail of the Kales Building, Detroit, 1998.*

182 *Derelict fast-food restaurant with vestigial paintings of a roasted chicken and a slab of ribs, South Central Los Angeles, 1997.*

183 *Derelict frame house with a sign warning arsonists, West Side of Detroit, 1995.*

182

183

184 *Section of the Wurlitzer Building, Detroit, 1996.*

185 *The People Mover traveling alongside the former Statler Hilton Hotel, downtown Detroit, 1998. The Statler Hotel, as it was originally called, was designed by the Beaux-Arts-trained architect George B. Post in 1914. The hotel closed around 1985.*

186 *View of the decayed east facade of the United Artists Building, downtown Detroit, 1998.*

184

185

186

187 *Detail of a triangular building, Harlem, 1997. The building is owned by one of Harlem's worst landlords. According to Ibo Balton, who works for the Harlem office of the Department of Housing Preservation and Development, the city "took the liberty to seal it to protect the public. Squatters have taken the wood from the ceiling. Kids go inside, there are a lot of kids in the neighborhood."*

188 *Ailanthus tree growing on a vacant Harlem building, 1995.*

188

189

189 *Cinderblocked windows of an 1890 apartment building, Harlem, 1999.*

190 *O'Dwyer Warehouse, Harlem, 1995.*

190

191

191 *Hat shop, Central Ward of Newark, 1980.*

192 *National Burlesque Theater, Detroit, 1998.*

192

194

193 *Entrance to Jacob Brothers Food Store, South Side of Chicago, 1997.*

194 *A high-tech seal by Rental Security Screens and Doors, made by the VPS company, South Side of Chicago, 1998.*

The Decoratively Sealed Building: "Not the Eyesore that It Was"

195

195 *Seal designed by the city of Newark for a window of the former South Park Calvary Presbyterian Church, 1998. As preservationist Liz Del Tufo explained, "They wanted to do anything that would make it more attractive, not such a boarded-up building."*

What if all those buildings by the expressways visible to so many drivers did not look abandoned? If a derelict structure in an otherwise occupied block got new artistic seals, would its cheerful facade help prevent the block from further deterioration? Does it matter that a hollow hulk is lurking behind the illusion of occupancy?

The seal-up programs of New York City, Newark, and Gary have gone beyond the simple goal of preventing squatters, vandals, and the natural elements from entering abandoned buildings. By dressing up a building, city officials hope to lure investors into fixing it. New York's Department of Housing Preservation and Development described it in 1982: "The 'Occupied Look' is a decorative tin seal-up program…aimed at improving the appearance of a neighborhood by applying vinyl decals with simulated window designs to all visible openings in selected vacant residential buildings."

New York City's was the largest of these programs. The early 1980s saw the decorative covering of tens of thousands of city windows. Critics saw those shiny decals with their awnings, flower pots, and curtains as an admission that the city was never going to fix the vacant buildings, that it had no intention of providing housing for poor and homeless families.

In downtown Gary, the city and a small seal initiative sponsored by the state's Department of Commerce Mainstreet Program sealed two buildings along Broadway. One of them was the Minnesota Building, a simple two-story red-brick structure with four storefronts. Before it became completely vacant in 1989 its last tenants were Downtown Grocery and Produce, 20th-Century TV, and the Palace Hat Shop. The other structure sealed was the Princess Theater. Prior to its "beautification," its entrance had been boarded up, and the windows above the marquee had been broken.

Gwen Bailey, head of Gary's Mainstreet Program, said: "We organized a contest throughout the city to dress up these

196

buildings. We wanted to keep the elements out, to make them presentable, to make them attractive to developers. We didn't want just to throw some boards on, we wanted to dress up those boards. We used grade-A exterior plywood. The cost of doing the two buildings was forty thousand dollars. We wanted to save them as an arts cluster and to bring in music stores and housing."

Broadway Beauty Supply shares a wall with the Minnesota Building. Linda, an employee there, admitted that the building looks "nice—something different." But she can hear it crumbling on the other side of the wall. Especially after a rain, she hears plaster falling. She says that the building has caught fire four times in seven years. Instead of spending money to make it look better, tearing it down seems preferable to her.

In 1997, the Princess Theater burned, and now the lot is empty. Although Gwen Bailey mentioned that there were some serious efforts underway, she did "not anticipate [the arts cluster] happening." She called the Mainstreet project "part of a movement to rehabilitate downtown" and characterized it as "somewhat of a success story."

196 *Building on the Grand Concourse sealed with "Occupied Look" plastic decals, South Bronx, 1986.*

197

198

199

200

197 *An abandoned block along Broadway, Gary, 1993.*

198 *The same stretch of Broadway after it was boarded up by Gary's Mainstreet Program, 1997.*

199 *Detail of the "fishbowl house," south side of Chicago, 1998. The decorations were painted by members of a nearby church.*

200 *Sealed apartment building, Central Ward of Newark, 1997.*

Interiors

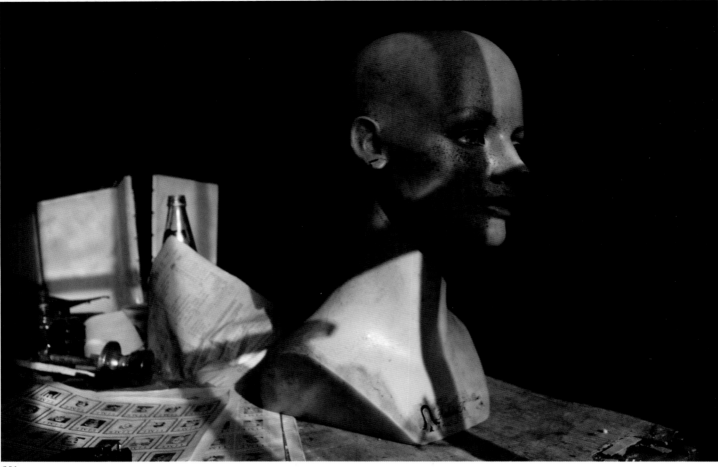

201

201 *Mannequin: "Nefertiti's sister," Robbins, 1995.*

Some objects inside of ruins are not worth the trouble to remove, break into pieces, and take to a junkyard. They stay behind. Among them are elevator doors, electric circuits, window frames, telephone books, and, often, old files. The carcass of an electric motor remains in place, while the copper from the machine is spooled out like a ball of thread and sold. Iron motors are too heavy and cheap for scavengers to break up their frames and carry them down dark stairways. Occasionally an odd presence is left behind, such as the large drum I once found containing biscuits and water to be consumed in the event of nuclear attack.

Homeless people bring to abandoned buildings the articles they need for day-to-day life: mattresses, chairs, tables, sofas, candles, plastic sealant to keep out the cold, and canned food. Strewn in rooms is an eclectic assortment of items, ranging from articles of clothing and empty food containers to stuffed animals, Bibles, porn magazines, and drug paraphernalia.

Objects such as children's car seats, strollers, and broken stereo sets are brought in and kept as potential capital. Sometimes homeless people drag a broken object into a vacant building with the intent to sell it only to find that the object is missing an important piece without which it has lost all value.

Historian Tim Samuelson comments on the objects left inside boarded-up Catholic churches in Chicago: "People who went to steal from abandoned churches didn't want to mess with the statues. They were not salable. They were not worth stealing, and if they were damaged it would bring the scavengers bad luck.

They remained in the building until the very end."

In a section of his junkyard at Star Auto Wreckers on the South Side of Chicago, Archie Humbert displays a collection of old religious statues. He calls it his "holy garden." Mr. Humbert explained how the head of a statue of the Virgin stays in place: "It has not fallen due to the mercy of the Lord. It is just sitting there, even though there has been wind, rain, and snow." Archie is not a Catholic, yet the statues give him "a spirit" and "an image," filling a void left when he gave up gambling. Statues like this come from demolished Catholic churches on the South Side of Chicago. Mr. Humbert "pulled the statues out of the mud as the equipment was running them over."

During a visit to Washington, D.C., in 1998, I saw on display at the Arts and Industry Building of the Smithsonian Institution a Lindy-Wolf Refrigeration Compressor taken from Baltimore's American Brewery (see chapter 1) in 1967, which was restored in 1975. As an officer at the Smithsonian Institution explained to me, "It could have been scrapped or sent into a junkyard. It was just happenstance that it ended up here." On my return to New York City, I stopped in Baltimore to visit the brewery. Lying on the ground floor was a discarded stuffed horse. I could not help comparing the splendid machine I had seen the day before in Washington with the toy on the floor. A curator had arranged to remove the piece for safekeeping and display in the nation's capital, and a scavenger had brought in a toy horse: two objects, two people, two Americas.

202

202 *Improvised bedroom in an abandoned office building, downtown Newark, 1989.*

203

204

205

206

203 *Stuffed toy horse left inside the American Brewery, East Baltimore, 1999.*

204 *Mailboxes in a semi-abandoned, high-rise part of the Horner Homes, Chicago, 1998.*

205 *Fragment of a toilet left in a Ninth Avenue apartment, Times Square area, Manhattan, 1995.*

206 *Section of a Ninth Avenue stairwell, Times Square area, 1995.*

207

207 *Rusting elevator equipment, United Artists Building, downtown Detroit, 1998.*

208 *The penthouse of the former Statler Hilton Hotel, Detroit, 1998. I call it "the Gallery of Machines," after Henry Adams's account of his visit to the Great Paris Exposition of 1900.*

208

209

209 *Archie Humbert's statue collection displayed in his junkyard, South Side of Chicago, 1997.*

210 *Archie Humbert's statue of the Virgin Mary, broken at the neck, South Side of Chicago, 1998.*

210

CHAPTER FOUR

Dealing with Eyesores

Its like a jungle sometimes
it makes me wonder
how I keep from going under (Huhh huh huh Huhh).
  —"The Message," Grandmaster Flash and the Furious Five

You'll think I'm crazy, but the houses began to speak to me.
  —Tyree Guyton

211 *Parking garage in the former Michigan Theater, downtown Detroit, 1995. The spirit of Piranesi lives in the pink and yellow Rococo interiors, which have been transformed with the addition of gray concrete platforms and cement ramps. The ornate shell has been severely truncated, and the ceiling is perforated, revealing the flimsy basis of its fantasy world. Rusted steel beams support the floors where cars are parked. As if celebrating the transformation, pigeons, sparrows, and starlings have made their home among the carved putti and nude young maidens and within the folds of the crimson curtains.*

The Rehabilitation of the Morrisania Hospital, South Bronx

The Morrisania Hospital complex, two blocks west of the Grand Concourse in the South Bronx, once contributed to the thoroughfare's magnificence. Designed in the 1920s by municipal architect Charles Meyers in a typically American scale and characteristically European style, the huge compound was landscaped to make a harmonious campus-like setting. Its eleven stories made it much higher than its surroundings.

In the late 1970s, the hospital complex was fenced-off, isolated, and decaying. The elegance of the yellow brick edifices and their rational spatial arrangement made them arresting as ruins. The bricks turned golden at sunset. Arched windows and loggias made the structure look like an enormous stage set. Huge trees rose from the open courtyard at the center. Occupying an entire block, the defunct hospital and its four ancillary buildings constituted the largest abandoned structure in the South Bronx.

In 1996 and 1997, the hospital's main building was rehabilitated as an apartment house with health, educational, and day-care facilities, and the ancillary buildings were demolished to make room for an elementary school and its playground. The project cost twenty-three million dollars.

After the hospital closed in 1978, the complex became an island where people down on their luck, depressed, insane, addicted, or temporarily homeless found asylum. It became their base of operations. At first the entrances to the hospital and the first-floor windows were cinderblocked and the perimeter fenced. Soon, sections of the fence were ripped and cinderblocks removed from the entrances. Squatters moved in. The hospital's fate suggests that sealing is part of a bureaucratic ritual that serves no practical purpose.

Many of the squatters did odd jobs for local building superintendents and merchants. Others were predators, however, who mugged neighborhood people and robbed the local stores. Their activities

212

213

214

215

212 *Morrisania Hospital under rehabilitation, South Bronx, 1996.*

213 *Morrisania Hospital, 1987.*

214 *Morrisania Hospital, 1998. The hospital is now rehabilitated as homeless housing, a cooking* *school, a catering establishment, and a bilingual school still under construction.*

215 *Main building of the Morrisania Hospital under rehabilitation, 1997.*

brought in the police, whose ineffectual searches disrupted everybody's lives.

Scavengers operated freely inside and around the building, stealing copper, aluminum, and bronze. Hundreds of broken fans, their blue plastic blades scattered on the ground and their hard bodies cracked like empty shells, attested to the energy and hard work that went into harvesting the copper.

I interviewed several squatters who said that they saw the former Morrisania Hospital as just a place to live. Some were related to each other and lived communally. Others were so wrapped up in their own worlds that, if addressed, they looked away and continued their monologues. Nobody seemed worried about finding another place to move to.

Manny, who had lived there eight years, told me he had made over two thousand dollars selling scrap metal from the buildings. The center of his life was his bedroom, in an elevator room of one of the smaller structures. His yard was the roof, and he was shaded by trees that had taken root there. He would wake up to the air filtering through the trees "smelling nice and fresh."

I met two black drug addicts, three Puerto Ricans, a mild mannered, homesick Nigerian, and a Cherokee. When Joe, one of the residents, showed me around the complex, he related that he had slept in every part of the compound. He answered my questions but avoided eye contact. He told me that he followed his grown children on the streets without being seen by them.

When someone broke into the car of one of the construction workers in 1996, the structures were resealed. This time, the workers made sure that the squatters could not get through. Pedro, an older Puerto Rican with a kind face who speaks a deep, clear Spanish, was the only person still allowed to live in the complex.

On a visit to the east wing after the resealing, I stumbled onto Pedro's home, in Blood Donors Room 203. It was a small

216

narrow room with a couch, and I smelled lard and saw rats scampering across the floor. In the semidarkness, the stench and the sight of so many rats were overwhelming. By the window, a blackened cauldron full of lard, which Pedro used for cooking, explained the rodents. In the room next door was his bed. Underneath it, the squeaking rats claimed it as their room too. Yet, the room was remarkably orderly and clean. Pedro's bed had been carefully made, and the room had three neatly arranged sections: a corner with empty liquor bottles; two rows of foodstuffs carefully stacked by the side of the bed; and, near the entrance, a corner with a broom and assorted cleaning utensils. A few wood sticks about a foot in length were for hitting the rats. It was too dark for me to compose my pictures. I photographed the room even though it was invisible to me.

In the basement I came across a sign that read MORTUARY. There was no trash here. Fear and darkness must have kept squatters away. I entered a large empty room with a white metal table and several rows of clear, empty jars aligned on shelves behind it. My flashlight was too small to illuminate the room, but the place seemed mostly bare. In a small room to the side, the floor was littered with test tubes. It made me think of the tens of thousands of cadavers that had entered and exited this room during the half century of the hospital's operation.

The architectural renderings of the projected rehabilitated main building portray thin, elegant people of uncertain race—multiculturalism meets the Roaring Twenties. I think of the families that now live in the building, and of the elementary school that will open on the southern half of the block. It is hard to tell how all this will hang together.

As I took one last look at the broken fans and their blue blades strewn on the

217

216 *Blood Donors Room, Morrisania Hospital, 1996.*

217 *Pedro's improvised bedroom in the Blood Donors Room, 1996.*

ground, at the arched windows and the golden yellow brick, I saw in my mind the strange glow coming from the rusting dissection table in the deep pit and heard the squeaking rats in the Blood Donors Room. Here, for a short time, I felt that the world was enchanted.

Morrisania Hospital was once a large, beautiful complex, and it subsequently became one of New York City's most alluring ruins. Now it has been reintroduced into the urban fabric. Rather than being razed and replaced by vacant land and parking lots, or townhouses, the structure has survived. One large and one small building have been restored. The space is useful again—to hundreds of South Bronx residents. But three of the buildings have been lost, and, with them, the campus quality, the harmonious arrangement of buildings, and their unity of purpose and style. Still, compared to the fate of so many notable buildings of the period, the former Morrisania Hospital has been a success story.

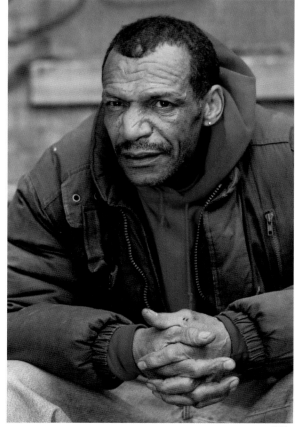

218 *Mortuary in the basement of the east wing of the Morrisania Hospital, 1996.*

219 *Joe Harris, resident of Morrisania Hospital, 1996.*

Police Youth Bureau, Detroit: Phoenix and Castle

The former Eighth Precinct Police Station, designed in 1900 by Louis Kamper, is located on Rose Parks Boulevard at the corner of Grand River Avenue. As a police building, it had a very bad reputation in the black community. According to Ken Jordan, a former community organizer, "The youth-gang squads used to arrest teenagers and bring them in there for questioning. There were many stories about it. This was primarily a white police force, and African-Americans were being arrested."

Located just a few blocks from the epicenter of the 1967 Detroit riots, the derelict station was a substantial ruin in an already devastated area. I regularly made portraits of the building, expecting its disintegration to continue, but my slides revealed subtle changes; I discovered that the plywood on the second-floor windows had been removed and replaced with new windows. The interior revealed more surprises: beautifully refurbished rooms with new floors, ceilings, and stairways. In 1998 a new tall iron fence encircled the building. Outside work was expected to start in the summer of 1999. The developers call the former station "Phoenix and Castle," after the mythical bird that rises from its own ashes (a favorite with developers) and in acknowledgment of the building's castle-like appearance. As for the station's bad reputation, Jordan remarked, "You don't allow that to influence you today. Things have changed now; our work is to rebuild. You don't forget, but you move on. People choose to move on and more forward."

221

220 *Police Youth Bureau undergoing a slow rehabilitation, 1998.*

221 *Entrance to Police Youth Bureau, 1997.*

Chicago Bee Building

222

The Chicago Bee Building took its name from the *Chicago Bee*, a well-known black newspaper on the South Side. Anthony Overton, a black tycoon who diversified a pioneering African-American cosmetics business into the fields of banking, insurance, and newspaper publishing, built it between 1929 and 1931. Often known as the "High Brown Man" because of his popular "High Brown Face Powder," Overton suffered a serious setback in 1929, forcing him to consolidate what was left of his businesses in the building. His family still had a beauty-supply store there until the mid-1980s, when the city bought it to make it into the Chicago Bee Branch Library.

City officials had been looking for a historic black landmark in the area to renovate for this purpose and chose the Bee Building because it had been continuously occupied and was in better shape than the other buildings under consideration. Unfortunately, soon after the city emptied the building of tenants, thieves ripped much of the Art Deco terra-cotta ornamentation off the front. Thefts like these are usually carried out by itinerant salvagers who, without ladders or sophisticated equipment, chip the heavy panels out from inside the building, taking the pieces that can easily be reached and leaving the rest behind. Loaded into car trunks and beat-up trucks, the pieces are then sold to dealers in architectural artifacts, who find ready resale from collectors and interior decorators.

When historian Tim Samuelson, who was working on the project for the Commission on Chicago Landmarks, asked a source about what should be done with ghetto landmarks, the response he received was "Knock them down, put a plaque on the side, they'll probably steal that too. Forget it, kid."

Samuelson frequented the city's salvage stores in Chicago in an unsuccessful search for the missing terra-cotta pieces. But then a 1991 photograph in *Chicago Magazine* about the city's salvage business caught his eye. Prominently displayed in the foreground was a terra-cotta piece of the Bee Building. He went to the store, where he found it priced at 125 dollars, and without saying anything to the owner, he registered a complaint with the South Side police. The police raided the store and transported the terra-cotta panel back to the station in the patrol wagon. The store owner said he had only one piece and that he had bought it for fifteen dollars from an itinerant salvager who went by the nick-name of "Greasy."

It turned out that Greasy had a considerable rap sheet for various criminal offenses, but the police claimed that they could not easily apprehend him, since he was reportedly living in his Cadillac. He eventually appeared at a police precinct on charges of beating his girlfriend. Greasy denied having any more terra-cotta pieces. At his trial, the judge and the prosecutor were both at a loss as to how to deal with terra-cotta theft. They released him. When Samuelson went to the precinct to retrieve the piece, the loudspeaker announced, "The guy has come to get the rock." On his way out, a policeman asked him, "Why do you care about that piece of shit?"

Tim Samuelson was afraid that the increased cost of remaking the other missing pieces would dissuade the city from restoring the building. Fortunately, the city decided to make the rest of the dozens of pieces at a cost of about 2,500 dollars each and completed the restoration of the Chicago Bee Branch Library.

223

224

222 *Chicago Bee Building, South Side of Chicago, 1986.*

223 *Chicago Bee Building, 1993.*

224 *Chicago Bee Building, 1995.*

225 *Chicago Bee Building, 1996.*

225

Krueger's Mansion, Newark: Lost Cause

226

226 *Gottfried Krueger Mansion, Newark, October 1981.*

227 *Krueger Mansion being rehabilitated as Newark's African-American Museum, 1998.*

228 *Classical bust at entrance to the Krueger Mansion, 1998.*

In Newark, the Krueger Mansion lies six blocks east of the site of the defunct former Krueger Brewery and about a mile northwest of Krueger's mausoleum. Over a period of eighteen years, my documentation of the three buildings that formed Gottfried Krueger's legacy raised issues of race, preservation, memory, and the stigma that repeated failure gives to a city landmark.

Krueger's commitment to Newark, expressed in the central location of these buildings, was not anomalous. At the turn of the century, other prominent members of the city's elite—such as John Fairfield Dryden, the founder of Prudential Insurance, and Peter Ballantine, an even more important brewer—also erected their businesses, homes, and tombs in the city. Today's Newark-area elite live in the sub-

urbs, and they identify neither their lives nor those of their families with the city.

The man who so strongly impressed himself on Newark's urban fabric had started as a penniless German immigrant, arriving in 1853 to work as an apprentice for five dollars a week in his uncle's brewery. The sixteen-year-old "lived in the homestead adjoining the brewery...and wore wooden shoes and a leather apron." By 1865, he was a partner in the brewery, one of the largest on the East Coast, and, in ten years, its sole owner. Krueger went on to become a New Jersey assemblyman, a judge, and a philanthropist. He established a hospital for sick and retired Germans and built a festival hall, Saengers Hall, for the city. His is the classic Horatio Alger story of "rags to riches."

In the early 1980s, some trees growing

227

on the brewery's roof—the tallest I had ever seen—attracted my interest. In 1987 the brewery complex, an old Victorian core flanked by modern buildings—was demolished to make space for a mall, which, it was promised, would bring a Shop Rite, two other large stores, and about four hundred permanent jobs to Newark's Central Ward. After the demolition, Councilman George Branch commented, "It was an eyesore, and as we begin to make economic progress in the ward, it needs to go." More than a decade later the land remains empty.

Krueger's mausoleum at Fairmount Cemetery was built in 1897 at the cost of 97,000 dollars. A large classical structure of Barre granite, it stands alone on a separate lot. Crossed torches on its facade are inverted to denote mourning, but on each corner of the building, large vessels contain

sculpted flames rising in the air. By the side of the altar, two life-sized angels are ready to soar.

In 1888 Krueger built a forty-three-room mansion on High Street for 250,000 dollars, the most expensive dwelling ever built in Newark. It had a bowling alley and a game room. Newark historian Charles Cummings interviewed a man who as a child had attended lavish dinners at the mansion and remembered that there was a footman behind each chair. The landmark building is listed on the national and the state registers of historic places.

The mansion later became the home and place of business of Louise Scott, the black owner of a cosmetology school and a chain of beauty salons. She lived there for a quarter of a century, until her death in 1983. Hers was also a rags-to-riches story. After

228

229

humble beginnings in domestic service, Mrs. Scott became Newark's first woman millionaire. Paul Stellhorn, a historian who wrote about Gottfried Krueger and his Newark, noted the similarities between Krueger and Mrs. Scott: both were entrepreneurs, both rose from very humble beginnings, and both were successes.

Unlike Krueger, however, Louise Scott died poor. Toward the end of her life, she sold important pieces of the mansion. A 1980 catalog published by the Los Angeles dealer John P. Wilson prominently depicted a "complete library of exotic German fruitwoods from the landmark Krueger Castle in Newark, New Jersey." In 1984, the *Bergen Record* reported that, before her death, Mrs. Scott's family sold many items, including stained-glass windows. In 1984 the "jewel of the Central Ward" was seized by the city for nonpayment of taxes, and the residents were evicted. The building was almost immediately vandalized.

In 1998, a sign outside the building read "Premier African-American Cultural Cen-

ter." Since 1990, Catherine Lenix-Hooker has presided over the project, the hoped-for reincarnation of one of Newark's most distinctive buildings as the "premier facility for the study and interpretation of the cultural arts and history of African-Americans in New Jersey."

In 1985 Edna Thomas of the Central Ward Coalition said, "We as a black people . . . have no place to hang our pictures." What would such a place look like? They set their sights on Mrs. Scott's former home. Under strict regulations for the use of state historic preservation funds, however, the mansion has increasingly become more Krueger's, more nineteenth-century, more German, and less black. Ms. Lenix-Hooker asked her critics to be patient. To those frustrated with the slow pace and expense of the work—more than seven million dollars in 1995—she answered, "I think people are going to stand back in awe once this whole project unfolds."

In early 1999, however, the priority was to find an additional two to four million dollars for bricks, fences, cast-stone

230

sidings, iron work, wallpaper, and furnishings that would match Krueger's originals and to pay the architects' fees and the wages of the skilled workers needed for rebuilding the interior. Grad Associates, the project architects, had already been paid 685,000 dollars. The mansion had been sitting empty for over a year, with nothing going on except for two security guards patrolling the premises. Meanwhile, people had grown frustrated that, after all the promises, so little had been done.

Of the plan to make the mansion into a cultural and artistic center, Andrew, the caretaker, commented, "Art in the ghetto: you need to move it [someplace safe]." He pointed to the nearby housing projects and to the enormous subsidized apartment building next door, which he called "the Beast," in relation to "Beauty," the mansion. To the suggestion that the building serve as the mayor's house, he replied, "The mayor would be scared as hell coming down here. There would be bodyguards all over."

Indeed, there is reason to worry. The mansion, in 1999, projects an aura of failure, and respectable people and institutions look the other way. After being heralded as the keystone of the battered Central Ward's revitalization, the landmark has become its pariah. With seven million dollars of public money already spent, the chief goal has become to ignore grandiose pronouncements, to save the building, and to make something useful out of it—a school, a day-care center, a home for the elderly, an apartment building, the mayor's house—anything. And to do it soon, before this landmark once again becomes a haven for winos and stray dogs. The shame would be to return to the mid-1980s, when the building was open, ransacked, vermin infested, and under the constant threat of arson. At this point it makes sense to just forget the cultural center, forget historic preservation, and forget the seven million dollars. I hope that new people with new ideas finish the job.

231 *Krueger mausoleum,
Fairmount Cemetery, Newark,
1987. The structure was designed
in 1897 by Gustavus Strehlin.*

232

Brooks Bakery, Harlem: Signs of the Times

232 *Posters on the boarded-up storefront of the Brooks Bakery, Harlem, 1993.*

A busy stretch of 125th Street between Park and Lexington Avenues—in a part of Harlem where tourists rarely venture—is flanked by two dubious landmarks: to the west, the nation's largest methadone clinic occupies three floors of an office building; to the east is the bus and subway stop where homeless people wait for a van to take them to a shelter on Randall's Island. A constant stream of the destitute flows past the vacant storefront of the old Brooks Bakery at number 111.

For years, the entrance was boarded up and plastered with posters, mostly featuring performers. Rappers came first, competing to appear mean, tough, and vulgar. A poster of Janet Jackson was accompanied only by the name "Janet" and her photograph. Upon seeing this photograph,

professor of political science Marshall Berman commented "We all know who Janet is. She is part of the family." Angela Bassett advertised the movie *What's Love Got to Do with It;* Oscar De La Hoya announced a boxing match; and, incongruously, Placido Domingo publicized the opera *Don Quixote.* Advertisements for horror movies appeared before Halloween. Once, when twenty posters depicting the face of a black boy were arranged in two orderly rows of ten each, Berman noted, "The face of the boy multiplied has a 'wanted poster' aura." The posters asked "Whose World Is This?"

For five years I photographed the facade of the former bakery, yet I never saw anyone admiring or even reading its advertisements. Nobody paid any attention

233

to me as I stood ready with my camera to incorporate passersby.

This was one of my preferred places to observe New York. Now the building is repaired, and its entrance has a pet store with a brand-new, silvery metal curtain, but no posters. I lost a place where, for a few seconds, popular art, the patterns of life it celebrated, and desperate people all came together.

234

233 *Brooks Bakery storefront, 1994.*

234 *Brooks Bakery storefront, 1995.*

235 *Brooks Bakery storefront, 1997.*

235

236

236 *Brooks Bakery storefront, 1998. New metal curtains announce the rehabilitation of the building. The posters are gone; the building no longer represents popular culture.*

237 *A pet store on the site of the Brooks Bakery, 1998.*

237

238

Firestone Tire Dealership, Detroit

The former Firestone Tire Dealership could have been one of the models in *Architectural Forum*'s special issue from the late 1940s, "New Buildings for 194x." The magazine published designs that exemplified the post–World War II democratic city, streamlined structures of glass, metal, and plastic, modern materials that were said to give form to people's aspirations and fit the tempo of the times. The architects writing in the issue wanted order, simplicity, plenty of green areas, and an abundant power supply. They rejected chaos, noise, monumentality, and decay—in other words, the dreary city of the past.

By 1993, the former tire dealership had already failed as a garage and as a hardware store, and the owner was planning to open a car wash. The building remained vacant

for a couple of years, was sold, demolished, and then replaced by Spin Cycle, part of a chain of laundromats operating in ghetto areas of Chicago and Detroit.

A sign painter named Eugene had made the signs for the hardware store phase of the former tire dealership. He made his living selling his services door-to-door on Detroit's West Side, and his style is distinctive: simple shapes, basic colors, and bold lettering. His repertoire consisted of a few simple objects: cars, tools, keys, houses, lawnmowers, and telephones. He used only saturated reds, blues, greens, yellows, and blacks. The cars he painted resemble wooden toy cars, with "ABC123" painted on their license plates. His telephones—black 1950s models—have receivers as large as a person and tiny bases. He often painted the base of buildings blue. On the facade of a long-gone video arcade I once saw a human face he had painted: a blue-eyed brown man with straight black hair and a Mexican mustache. Eugene liked stars and placed them against the background of his multicolored letters.

For a few years, the sweeping curves and white enamel surfaces of the International Style tire dealership provided Eugene with a canvas for his simple and equally restrained forms, but when the building became a rubbish container, signs faded, the outside panels fell, and big black openings replaced the facade's once brilliant white. Now the site is occupied by Spin Cycle, a small, one-story cinderblock structure fronted by a parking lot. The building could be featured in an issue entitled "New Ghetto Buildings for 200x: Constructing the Lesser City."

The laundromat is certainly more useful to local residents than the decaying old Firestone Tire Dealership I first encountered in 1993. It was a wreck of a fine modern building, which was not going to last much longer. Eugene's work had brought new life to the exterior, but he did not complete the job. During its last days, as the panels fell away, the city posted on the facade a sign depicting a pair of eyes warning trespassers to keep away. Watching the structure fall apart was like seeing the future decay. It left me longing for progress and the spirit of Eugene.

239

238 *Firestone Tire Dealership, West Side of Detroit, 1993.*

239 *Firestone Tire Dealership, 1997.*

240 *A new cinderblock building going up on the site of Firestone Tire Dealership, 1997.*

241 *A laundromat called Spin Cycle in place of the Firestone Tire Dealership, 1998.*

240

241

242

In September 1998, Secretary of Housing and Urban Development Andrew Cuomo called for the destruction of "concrete bunkers, high-rise buildings that literally imprisoned and caged people." A federally sponsored housing transformation program named Hope VI had been created in 1993 to reshape public housing by demolishing as many as one hundred thousand units in the "nation's worst public housing projects." They were replaced by smaller, mixed-income developments. As Pam Belluck wrote in a September 1998 *New York Times* article, "On a scale not seen in decades, the Federal Government is helping cities to clear slums again, but this time they are the slums it helped create: public housing projects crippled by flawed policies and mismanagement and overwhelmed by poverty and crime."

In the 1950s and 1960s, what are today called "concrete prisons" were widely regarded as the solution to crowded cities. *Architectural Forum*'s January 1952 issue stated that "a tower of apartments in an open park furnishes a far better way of life than a warren of houses or walk-ups congesting a site." Architects were challenged to create above-ground communities with "sidewalks in the sky," "tot lots in the air," and "play corridors" and "neighborhoods" on each floor. In the space below, landscaped trees and gardens would form parks between the towers.

Number 2051 West Lake Street, a medium-rise building in the Henry Horner Homes, was one such community. Designed in 1957 by Skidmore, Owings & Merrill on Chicago's West Side, the edifice exemplified the rational spirit of Ludwig

Mies van der Rohe and his followers. Through Hope VI the hulk and three other apartment buildings—what once was seen as the future—have been demolished and replaced by more than three hundred units of rental housing. New Victorian-style three-story townhouses with pitched roofs stand in contrast to the surrounding semi-abandoned high-rises. The goal is to create a community of residents with mixed incomes. The situation seems unstable—a mix of high-rise projects, depopulation, and some isolated developments, for example, a new stadium, a new public library, and a new community center.

As the modernist architects had predicted, most of the land surrounding the townhouses was cemented for roads, sidewalks, and entranceways, leaving little space for individual lawns. Officials claim that the townhouses bring back the housing types that existed before the high-rises, implying that the urban fabric will be restored to its pre-1950s condition. But to the south lies the United Stadium, the site of the 1995 Democratic National Convention, a huge structure surrounded by acres of parking lots; to the north is a former industrial area of primarily razed or abandoned factories; and to the east and west lies the legacy of two riots and forty years of disinvestment.

Official pronouncements about the demolition of the projects blamed the style and type of construction of the buildings themselves, but the real cause is political: the city's policy of concentrating the poorest of the poor, the people with the most acute social problems, in these developments. That is what made these projects represent the worst in ghetto living. As highly visible symbols of despair, the high-rises were easy to identify and demolish.

243

244

242 *2051 West Lake Street, Henry Horner Homes, Chicago, 1995. Upon seeing the photograph, a resident of the city commented that the building was "weeping."*

243 *View east along West Lake from Oakley, 1989.*

244 *View east along West Lake from Oakley, 1998.*

Chicago Pinks

245

Occasionally I have seen people gathering bricks from abandoned buildings at demolition sites in Brooklyn and Newark, but this activity is much more common in Chicago, where ordinary bricks used for the sides and the back of buildings were made from local clay. According to historian Tim Samuelson, the fired bricks have a "beautiful pink, unlike the bricks made in other cities. That is why people call them 'Chicago pinks.' These bricks are considered very exotic by interior designers and architects who want interior walls to get that beautiful pinkish buff color." He adds that nobody wants the fancy bricks from the facade.

In Chicago, where the pinks are taken for granted, there is no demand for them, except for occasional repair work. At demolition sites all over the city, crews arrange the bricks on pallets, putting cardboard and metal straps over them, and send them to places like Florida, Texas, and California. "We are all professional brick cleaners around here. We get ten dollars a box, about forty to fifty a day depending on how hard you work and the condition of the bricks. You call the company and they tell you where the new job is," said Habib, who worked at a demolition site in Woodlawn for the Windy City Antique Brick Company.

245 *Recycling Chicago pinks from the demolition of Tempo Howard Industries, Lawndale, Chicago, 1990.*

246 *Recycling bricks from a six-flat apartment building, Woodlawn, Chicago, 1998.*

247 *Recycling bricks from the Woodlawn Methodist Church, South Side of Chicago, 1998.*

246

247

248 *Fading image of crucified Christ, talking, with his eyes wide open, on the Crossover Inner City Gospel Ministry, Cass Corridor, Detroit, 1998.*

Art that is specific to urban ruins is generally perceived as a positive contribution: a way to disguise the scars of fires and vandalism, to affirm private and collective identities, and to vent rage. Artists frequently create symbols of their history, of the ordeals they have gone through, and of their accomplishments in their devastated neighborhoods. The site-specific art sets up another level of discourse on the cityscape and its destruction.

Sometimes, preserving buildings and producing art are part of the same struggle. "Artists find something energizing and electrifying in cityscapes of increasing disorder and entropy. They want to pick up the pieces, to fight large economic forces, to bear witness, to resist the image of collapse," says John Beardsley, a professor of landscape architecture. By making a shrine of a building, artists can help save it until a developer or the city steps in to refurbish it. When officials threaten to raze a structure, local activists rally in support of it and its works of art. An early example of this was William Walker's 1960s *Wall of Respect*. It consisted of a group of portraits of famous African-Americans and their most memorable sayings painted on the plywood panels that sealed the upper stories of a vacant building on the South Side of Chicago. During the 1980s in the South Bronx, there was another way of using exalted symbols to save apartment buildings. The ruin of one building, for example, had motifs of African royalty, lions, and masks painted on its facade. It has been rehabilitated.

Mural portraits of Martin Luther King, Nelson Mandela, and Malcolm X facing blighted and empty lots are so common in the inner city that it raises questions regarding the connection between these icons and the ruins that surround them. In contrast, monumental portraits of tough-looking drug dealers who display guns and oversized beepers fit very well on the street corners where they once spent long hours selling dope.

248

249

250

249 *"Black Pantheon" with former Chicago mayor Harold Washington at center right, West Side of Chicago, 1990.*

250 *Black Pantheon fades, 1994.*

251 *Almost invisible Black Pantheon, 1998.*

251

Particularly deadly fires are often commemorated with painted portraits of the victims, accompanied by their names, dates of birth and death, and sometimes even their toys, clothing, and school photographs. Neighbors feel the need to come to terms with the sudden tragedy by placing notes at the site, creating impromptu bulletin boards.

Graffiti covers a wide range of expression. Often, writings express anger, such as the destructive desire expressed by the phrase scrawled in several places in downtown Detroit, "Killing Hoez all day. Only Nigga Hoez," and the ubiquitous "Fuck the World." Other messages are moving because of their spontaneity, bitter honesty, and unlikely placement. On the second floor of a vacant ABLA townhouse in Chicago, I read this manifesto: "Me and Ko Ko is departed again but this time for the Better to become SOBER couples Husband wife Every Body Hoping that we fell and become homeless again But STAY TUNE EVERY BODY."

In notorious urban areas such as the South Bronx, improved conditions are obviating the need for "art on the edge." As political science professor Marshall Berman observed in his essay "Views from a Burning Bridge," "A great burst of creativity emerged from the Bronx's ruins, and it deserves remembrance and celebration. But in fact most art grows out of normality. As the Bronx starts a new millennium, it will have a chance to nourish less desperate modes of creativity, and we can look forward to celebrating those."

252

252 *Outdoor display on the exterior wall of an abandoned building featuring African-American motifs by "Dream Keeper," South Side of Chicago, 1995.*

253

253 *Expanded outdoor display on the wall of the same abandoned building, South Side of Chicago, 1997.*

254 *Mural on an abandoned building, executed "In Memory of Wil," South Camden, 1997. The portrait of a homeboy is done with the elegance and vigor of a nineteenth-century Japanese Kabuki print.*

254

255

256 *Portrait drawn on a bathroom cabinet of the former Scudder Homes, Central Ward of Newark, 1987.*

256

The Heidelberg Project, Detroit: Tyree Guyton's "Illegal Junkyard"

257 *The "Fun House" on Heidelberg Street, dressed up by artist Tyree Guyton and bulldozed by the city in 1991, East side of Detroit, 1991.*

In the 3600 block of Heidelberg Street in Detroit, orphaned objects find orphaned houses. The neighborhood, dotted with one- and one-and-a-half-story frame houses, is reminiscent of the typical American neighborhood, but since the late 1980s, artist Tyree Guyton has been attaching the detritus of everyday life all over the walls and roofs of abandoned houses: a multitude of broken, dismembered, and bruised objects, stuffed animals, dolls, and tires. As a resident of Mount Elliot Avenue once explained to me, "We have this artist here, his name is Tyree. He does this sort of thing with dolls and shit. He is world famous, but pay no attention to it; we are good people here." He covers vacant lots with worn shoes and clusters of upright car hoods spray-painted with smiley faces. Tyree's visual language is coherent, however. Recurring motifs include polka dots, smiley faces, crosses, and the word "God." The familiar place names on recovered street signs peek out from layers of sundry accretions. Looking at a section of the Heidelberg Project, people may at first be amused by the surreal juxtaposition of objects, but there is a decidedly sinister side to his creations. He uses red paint liberally on his mannequins and dolls, suggesting that a massacre has taken place.

Sometimes Tyree makes forays outside his immediate territory into nearby streets. He dressed up a two-story frame house with large classical columns on Mount Elliot Avenue by putting political campaign ads all over it; he called the finished product "The White House." A mannequin's head was positioned within the space once occupied by an oval window in the pediment gable. There it now dangles, slowly rotating.

Not all neighbors are happy to see their surroundings covered with discarded and spray-painted objects. They have asked visitors, "Would you like this stuff next door to you?" One neighbor complained that after a rain the stuffed animals

257

smelled foul. Nobody asked local residents if they would prefer to have their abandoned houses look as they did before, with dark holes instead of windows, garbage-stuffed entrances, charred exteriors, and the ubiquitous anti-arson symbol provided by the city: a pair of wide-open eyes next to words that say "This building is being watched." City officials have tried to discourage Tyree by fining him for littering and by demolishing the houses and, with them, his work.

Mel Washington, a developer asked: "What is the difference between that and a junkyard? A junkyard should not impact on the surrounding area. A lot of people say, 'This is the stuff that we try to get rid of when we see it in our streets and alleys, and it should be treated as junk.' We don't memorialize stuff like that. His supporters should buy the land and he should get a permit for a junkyard and put an eight-foot screen fence around his place."

A fence would surely dilute the impact of the Heidelberg Project, which comes from catching people by surprise. People have become accustomed to driving through devastated streets without looking at them. Tyree Guyton has made them visible again.

Furthermore, the Heidelberg Project has made a dangerous, marginal area of Detroit safer. Crime, drugs, and prostitution have gone elsewhere. Crack houses and shooting galleries have closed. Tyree's supporters portray his work as one of Detroit's main attractions, a draw for thousands of visitors to the city.

Since his assemblages are exposed to the elements, Tyree's work is always in flux. The city has demolished several—four of them on a single Saturday in the fall of 1991. The city also ordered Tyree to denude his houses and undress his trees and vacant lots by August 1998. His fans protested by putting dots on abandoned buildings all over Detroit. The statue

258 *Dressed-up house, part of the Heidelberg Project, 1991.*

259 *"The White House," Heidelberg Project, 1998.*

259

261

known as the *Spirit of Detroit*, the symbol of the city, got one too.

It is difficult to imagine that Tyree's houses will be undecorated any time soon. It would require much of his tremendous energy to dismantle the project, and he is more likely to create new work than to take down what he has wrought. The city will probably continue to demolish his pieces. But by "dotting" Detroit, Tyree's admirers will at least keep alive the memory of the Heidelberg Project. While city administrators concentrate on downtown development and gambling casinos, Tyree Guyton keeps attention on the ongoing plight of the city's poorer neighborhoods.

I visited Heidelberg Street in September 1998, expecting to see the houses demolished and the objects removed. Amazingly they were still there, along with many visitors and several new displays. I overheard the artist telling one of the visitors who wanted to speak to him: "I can't talk to you now, I am in transition. I have to prepare for the transition." With that he strode off and paced his block like a caged panther.

Physically, little had changed when I returned to the project in late December 1998. Tyree Guyton had just returned from showing his work in Europe. Smiling, he was asking visitors to sign a guest book. He now owned two of his decorated houses, and, since the empty lots across the street are in private hands, he believed that the city was powerless. He invited me to check out his web site and turned to his other visitors.

The story of the Heidelberg Project continues, however. In February 1999, the city again raided his site, demolished his art warehouse, and removed his stuffed animals, television sets, dolls, and shoes from the trees and empty lots. Among the artists asked to comment on this by the *Detroit News*, Kristin Bly of Cleveland said: "I know the reality of putting things where others think they don't belong. Somehow the community can't accept the idea that one man's trash is another's treasure." Tyree's comment was much briefer. "I am in pain," he said, and promised to expand the project citywide.

260   *Boarded-up entrance to a house marked with one of Tyree Guyton's polka dots, 1998.*

261   *"Laughing Faces," Heidelberg Project, 1998.*

262

263

262 *Car, Heidelberg Project, 1991.*

263 *Grotesque torture scene on Heidelberg Street, 1992. A woman artist found this image "pretty disturbing."*

264 *Thousands of discarded shoes in a large empty lot, part of the Heidelberg Project, 1998.*

Bicentennial, Camden

265 *Bicentennial murals on the walls of abandoned buildings, Camden, 1982.*

I first photographed some crudely painted scenes of the Revolutionary War on the walls of abandoned buildings along Broadway in Camden in 1979. They had been made in the bicentennial year 1976. This display of patriotism by young black and Puerto Rican artists seemed odd to me, since the Emancipation Proclamation of 1863 had been so late in coming. It seemed even stranger to find these paintings juxtaposed with such wrecked buildings.

According to Art Thomson of Camden's Department of Health and Human Services, the project was intended as neighborhood beautification. For their murals the artists selected "viable surfaces that could be seen from a thoroughfare." Kathy Dumbar, who works in community relations for the city of Camden, told me that

she had participated in many of the community groups that created the murals and that there had been vocal dissent among the participants. "Some groups felt that the Bicentennial did not represent us because we didn't get our freedom until 1863. We were still enslaved in 1776, and the native Americans were still losing their land. But the majority argued that we were part of this country, and that we had helped to build it, so we decided to participate in the celebration." She went on to explain how "we got our stuff in those old, beat-up buildings": "Nineteen seventy-six came after the days of Black Power, and we were trying to hold on to something. We said, 'Here we are and this is our representation.' We painted in a bunch of ruins. We did not have the tall ships and all that great stuff

that they have. You saw some semblance of representation of our history on abandoned stores on Broadway, some semblance of the oppression, something at least. But ruins are not a good place to portray your history. We got a little history here and our history started crumbling. It ended up in being nothing. We need to do something more lasting. I would never push for something like that unless it was done in a lasting place and in a lasting manner."

I returned again and again to my color slides of these murals, asking myself what made them so powerful. The images represent almost forgotten events that had taken place in the mid-1970s as well as in the 1700s and 1800s. At the time of the Bicentennial, ghetto children had openly discussed whether they should join in and celebrate American independence. They felt ambivalent, and many opted out. The discussion, the crude icons selected for the murals, and their placement on derelict storefronts along Broadway made the celebration that they concocted a classic commentary on contemporary race relations. I envision this taking the form of a children's book, a proud publication issued by my imaginary Smithsonian of Decline.

266 *Bicentennial mural, 1979.*

267 *Vacant buildings used for Camden's bicentennial celebration, 1982.*

268

268 *"Your Mother," part of a public-service ad campaign, on a billboard, Central Ward of Newark, 1995.*

On New Year's Day 1995 in the Central Ward of Newark, I saw the first of many billboards depicting the solitary but anguished hollering face of a young black man placed horizontally along with a line of text. The image was unforgettable, and its location, among the abandoned buildings and empty lots, acknowledged a national tragedy just where it was most intensely felt. The billboard, like a patch, seemed to be holding together the derelict structures supporting it.

I saw the face as I traveled to Chicago, Detroit, and New York City. The billboards came with two different texts. I preferred the one with the words "Your mother" in large letters at the top. I interpreted the phrase as referring to all that had once been nurturing: the neighborhood, the buildings, the people, even the earth itself. For a while

I ignored the rest of the sentence, but below the face the text continued ". . . Didn't raise you to be a drunk." The other version said, "Dead men can't jump," with "Don't drive drunk" below the image.

This was not a work of environmental art in the tradition of Robert Smithson, Jenny Holzer, Barbara Kruger, or Dennis Hollier. I had come across an ad campaign, a public-service announcement designed to discourage young black men from excessive drinking. The ads were sponsored by Coors Brewery, Vibe, the Box, and Black Entertainment Television and designed by Uniworld Group, a New York–based, black-owned advertising agency. These billboards had long been rented for beer advertisements for Coors, and Coors donated the remainder of their leases to this extraordinary example of shock advertising.

269

270

271

272

Ghettos are full of glamorous images that encourage people to drink and smoke. Designers at Uniworld Group and black community leaders in New York City emphasized that alcoholism among young black males was a serious problem, and the signs were designed to grab the attention of this group. This campaign, they felt, was a step in the right direction. In explaining the selection of ghettos for the placement of the signs, Byron Lewis, the chairman of Uniworld, stated, "We were not hired to communicate to the white community."

It is doubtful that such signs would have been allowed in more affluent black or mixed neighborhoods. They were yet another symbol that visually defined ghettos, giving a symbolic cry to the most desolate of them. The billboards are gone, but I can still imagine a chorus of piercing screams coming from hundreds of huge open mouths all hollering together.

273

269 *"Your Mother," Newark, 1995.*

270 *"Your Mother," West Side of Detroit, 1995.*

271 *"Your Mother," Newark, 1995.*

272 *"Your Mother," Harlem, 1995.*

273 *"Your Mother," Newark, 1995.*

Swimming against the Tide

Me and old Newark are history. There are just a few crumbs left here and there.
   —Kea Tawana, contemplating the ruins of Murphy Varnish, Newark

Generally, only new and whole things tend to be considered beautiful; the old, fragmentary, and faded are thought to be ugly. What is rooted in thousands of years of perception—namely, the priority of youth over age—cannot be eliminated in a few decades.
   —Alois Riegl

What do we value in this culture?
   —Howard Gillette, American historian

274 *A tree growing from the roof of a building at the American Brewery complex, East Baltimore, 1999.*

275

275 *The People Mover circling the skyscraper graveyard, Grand Circus Park, Detroit, 1995.*

In 1980, J. B. Jackson published his famous essay "The Necessity for Ruins." Jackson concludes his piece by stating:

> But there has to be that interval of neglect, there has to be discontinuity; it is religiously and artistically essential. That is what I mean when I refer to the necessity for ruins: ruins provide the incentive for restoration and for a return to origins. There has to be (in our new concept of history) an interim of death or rejection before there can be renewal and reform. The old order has to die before there can be a born-again landscape . . . The old farmhouse has to decay before we can restore it and lead an alternative life style in the country; the landscape has to be plundered and stripped before we can restore the natural ecosystem; the neighborhood has to be a slum before we can rediscover it and gentrify it. That is how we reproduce the cosmic scheme and correct history.

The brand-new Colonial Villages, Pioneer Villages, Frontier Villages, and Army Posts of J. B. Jackson's small-town America are utterly foreign to me. Can ghettos too, like small towns, become with time "places where we can relive the golden age and be purged of historical guilt"? I have yet to see people leading an alternative lifestyle in Gary, or gentrifiers in Camden, or ecosystems being restored in West Pullman, Chicago. The golden age of the urban environments depicted in this book belonged to people who left them for the suburbs and show few signs of returning. These urban cores are, in the words of geographer Manuel Castells, the backwaters of the world economy, the "devalued spaces in the inner city . . . neglected places which the information highway and the space of flows have bypassed."

The places I document are mostly waning. Anyone embarking on a documentation project similar to *American Ruins* in the twenty-first century would be surveying a different landscape. Some of America's grandest derelict structures have been demolished. Gone are the Jack Frost Sugar Refinery in Philadelphia, several of the buildings that formed Camden's RCA complex, and most of the former world headquarters of Sears on Chicago's West Side. In Detroit, Hudson's Department Store was razed in 1998. The once common mile-long stretches of vacant structures along commercial streets have acquired a rural look after so much demolition. Occasionally new high-rises have been built amid the emptiness of large fenced plots of land, and

276

276 *Book Building, Detroit, 1998. Uneasily positioned above the grimy classical columns on top of the sinister building are two large white drums (outdated microwave transmitters), a forest of antennas, and the nests of peregrine falcons.*

277 *Shopping cart containing the possessions of a Mexican immigrant, South Central Los Angeles, 1998.*

277

commercial franchises have been erected in the middle of parking lots. Sprinklings of suburban-type developments are also found among the ruins.

RETURNING TO DOWNTOWN DETROIT

From homeless person to professor, there is unanimity among Detroiters that skyscrapers have no future as ruins. My proposal of keeping twelve square blocks south and west of Grand Circus Park as an American Acropolis—that is, to allow the present skyscraper graveyard to become a park of ripe ruins—is seen by most as at best misguided and at worst a cruel joke. When I tried to convince James, a homeless man, that ruins can be magnificent, he disagreed, saying that the area "is more like an eyesore." Another homeless man named Kenneth remarked: "The tempo of this city is to keep moving. If the ruins stay in the way of where they are going to put certain things, they are going to tear them down." He seemed surprised that I asked for his opinion, but homeless people in their wanderings are the real denizens of this area.

Ruins need fixing, Kelvin, a maintenance man, told me. To prove that downtown Detroit is not ruined he made a list: "We have Cobo Hall, we have the Festival, we have Canada, and we have the casinos." And he succinctly explained the difference between ruins here and those in Europe: "Them are ancient." Gary Sands, an urban planner at Wayne State University, responded to my proposal by saying: "This is an embarrassment to us; we don't make ruins, we make wonderful things." Ruins do not fit the optimistic outlook that prevails in Detroit.

Chicago historian Tim Samuelson warned me about the special impermanence of modern ruins. He said that traditional ruins like those of Rome or Pompeii have endured because they were built brick upon brick and the force of gravity helps hold them together. Modern buildings are constructed more like stage sets, held together by clips and clamps. Water degrades the whole building; moisture seeps in, masonry disappears. "You have a problem when pieces start falling from twenty stories high; it presents a challenge to preserve them as ruins." Buildings open up, become like bird cages, rusty skeletons.

Can periodic observations of Detroit's old skyscrapers help identify trouble spots so that they can be fixed before people get hurt? Detroit officials are already protecting the public by placing barriers on the sidewalk across from the former Book-Cadillac Hotel and scaffolding and warning signs on the Metropolitan Building. The cladding of these buildings would probably take centuries to shed. In the process, ever new and surprising aspects of their semicovered skeletons would emerge, opening perspectives right through them. Trees and bushes would give these enormous human-made mountains a covering of nature, changing in color with the passing of the seasons.

The skyline of Detroit has thinned out and receded. Its width has become narrower with the elimination of the YMCA building and nearby hotels to the east, and the implosion of Hudson's Department Store has left a big gap at the center. I can foresee a massive demolition of the old downtown, with the Kales Building as the remaining token structure—the one tall and elegant landmark left to recall the former glory of Grand Circus Park. I can imagine Detroit losing its pre-Depression skyline.

Yet I am unable to give up the vision of an American Acropolis. What is a ruined skyscraper if not an impressive structure? Would twelve square blocks of ruins forever compromise the future of Detroit, a city of 140 square miles? Why can't the planned rebuilding take place *around* the ruins, as it has in Rome? Are these towering structures just dead things, mere symbols of deindustrialization and economic decline? In reality, they are the symbols of what led this nation into the twentieth century, and they will soon become invisible. In downtown Detroit, as in Rome, it is still possible to marvel at the crumbling of such essential pieces of urban history. Are these not places where we can meditate on progress?

DECLINE AND EVERYDAY LIFE

Unlike recent celebrated buildings, which are cold and distant in their perfection, derelict structures form some of our most moving urban spectacles. But their dramatic quality and extraordinary beauty are often lost on local residents. Understandably, they see in them a reflection of how bad things have gotten in their community and would like them fixed or demolished.

The growing frustration over ruins that "just stand there" was epitomized in a front-page article in the *Detroit News* by reporter Cameron McWirther, a critique of Mayor Dennis Archer's disastrous handling of the snow removal operation after a severe blizzard in January 1999. Illustrating the article was a grotesque image of the Ransom Gillis Mansion in Brush Park, which, according to McWirther, "stood as a symbol of Detroit's difficulty in tearing down the abandoned buildings that pockmark the city." With some photographic manipulation, what to me is a magnificent ruin became an image representing the shame of a city where nothing seems to work.

Few people admit that the buildings in which they live or work are actually ruins. A former headstone showroom in Detroit has its wraparound windows sealed and painted white, and its front yard is overgrown, giving the impression that it has been

mothballed. Above its entrance, against black marble, is a fading gold star. Yet someone in the building answered the phone and responded to my questions by saying: "I work on cars. I'm very busy right now." Left to decide whether or not the building was a ruin, I took another look at the faded gold star against the black polished stone and decided that it was.

In 1996 I asked a man looking out the window from a semi-abandoned South Bronx tenement if his building was a ruin. His reply: "This is not a ruin, this is my home. If you don't like it, lend me money to fix it." The manager of the former Packard Plant stressed that the complex was an architectural masterpiece, a glory of Detroit, and threatened to sue me if I even hinted that it was a ruin.

Even though viewed as doomed, some ruined structures continue to elicit interest and loyalty because of their sheer presence and the good memories associated with them. "Victim" buildings such as these are singled out in small spontaneous gestures of recognition. Brooklyn's Bushwick Theater, for example, has long been left behind, yet an image of the building when it was new was featured on a 1999 calendar sponsored by the Brooklyn borough president, and a detail of it in its ruined state is included in *The Neighborhoods of Brooklyn*, a 1998 book edited by John B. Manbeck. The theater was renamed Pilgrim Baptist Cathedral and served as a sanctuary for more than a decade.

280

279 *Monument showroom, later a produce store and a car wash, and now a garage, Detroit, 1998.*

280 *"The Salvation Army, Erected A.D. 1928 to the Glory of God and the Good of Humanity," Benton Harbor, Michigan, 1998. The building is boarded up, but the flag of prospective tenants is already flying.*

Pilgrim Baptist's Bishop Brown told me that the edifice was merely "a building that we used for a period of time, and that was it. Then we bought another piece of property nearby." As for the extraordinary plaster putti on the theater's facade, Bishop Short explained, "We didn't put that on the building. That was already there when we came. We don't believe in angels."

In the case of Newark's grand Calvary Presbyterian Church, only the columned facade stands. Perceived as a hopeless case, the structure nevertheless projects an aura. When a work crew sealed it, they felt compelled to paint a cross on two of the boarded-up windows. And former addicts from Integrity House, a nearby drug-rehabilitation program, keep the large planters on the church's front steps filled with red flowers.

A discarded airplane lying on a heap of old cars in a Los Angeles junkyard elicited a painted question from an anonymous graffiti artist: "Will it ever fly?" The junkyard's owner issued a verdict: "It is not a plane anymore; now it is a piece of junk." When passersby see a broken and discarded Mickey Mouse, a derelict International Harvester fire truck, or an extinguished neon sign, they instinctively decide whether they would like to see such cast-offs saved, fixed, or sold for profit.

Goth rockers from the Chicago area frequent the former City Methodist Church in Gary. Goths dye their hair black, wear leather and chains, put on dark eye makeup, and

281 *Kea Tawana on the grounds of the Essex County Jail, Newark, 1999.*

282 *Kea Tawana inside the Essex County Jail, Newark, 1999.*

grow long fingernails. As preservationist Chris Meyers explained, "They like to stand silently near the altar, enjoying the life that the building has. They don't bother anybody. It is hard to find spirituality in your parents' suburban basement."

Even though global social and economic forces have caused the abandonment and ruination of cities, those forces do not determine the forms that decline will take. Stories of abandonment are as unique as the stories of the people involved in them. For example, the corner of 97 Hinkley Street in Benton Harbor, Michigan, is so still that it would be hard to find a place that looks more desolate. At the center is a boarded up Gothic citadel, a two-and-a-half-story former Salvation Army building of dark brown brick—an impressive structure. Captain Halloway, the present head of the organization, doesn't know the reason his predecessors "pulled back" from 91 Hinkley and moved a couple of blocks away, to a former funeral home. He "now questions the wisdom of it." I puzzled over the meaning of the triangular flag waving atop the citadel decorated with figures that I took to be Roman soldiers.

"The building was erected by the Salvation Army and was occupied by it until 1963 when they walked away from the whole thing," said Scott Elliot, a former art dealer from Chicago who, with his wife Eileen Cropley, is behind an effort to rehabilitate it. What I had interpreted as ancient warriors on the flag were in fact dancers. Elliott and Cropley plan to convert the citadel into a dance school and studio, part of an effort to change the image of the community through the arts. "It is a fine building; it has big open spaces and an auditorium," said Cropley. "The building has a presence," added Elliott. "The rehabilitation is going to happen. In fact, I am positive that is going to happen."

KEA TAWANA: THE ARK BUILDER
RETURNS TO VISIT THE GHOSTS OF NEWARK

While revisiting in early 1999 a site I had photographed in the South Bronx, I was surprised to see my friend Kea Tawana threading through the crowds on Third Avenue. She was taking pictures with the kind of camera subscribers to *Time* receive. I had thought she was dead. "I thought you were dead, too," she told me.

Kea opened her mouth to show me she had lost all her teeth. She said that she had been living in a hole in Prospect Park, Brooklyn, for four months. She had left food there, but she thought it would be spoiled. In any case, she was now renting a room in Brooklyn.

I suggested we go to Newark. She agreed. We visited the ruins of the Essex County Jail. The chain and lock on the main door fooled me into believing there was no way to get in, but Kea found another entrance. Formerly an inmate at the jail in Caldwell, New Jersey, she found it ironic to return to prison. Her eyes, trained by decades of scavenging, found century-old nails, a cigarette lighter shaped like a gun, and the carcass of a dog. She examined the locks on the jail doors and wished she had a torch to cut them loose. In an antique shop, she told me, locks like these would fetch at least one hundred dollars apiece.

I sensed that Kea was eager to return to the place where for six years she had built an ark. Her splendid vessel, set on a high point in Newark's Central Ward, had been ninety feet long and thirty feet high. "That was the new ark of hope; that is why I had to build it so big," she said. Erected with the discarded fragments of old Newark, the boat attracted visitors from all over the country but also the unrelenting hostility of local officials, who saw it as an eyesore. The city forced her to dismantle it in 1988. When I

283

asked whether she hoped to rebuild it, she said: "There isn't any other ark in me." She told me she was afraid her visit would give her nightmares.

At the ark site Kea looked downward and remarked how a tree she had last seen as a potted plant was now one foot in diameter. She looked for a tombstone engraved with the name of the founder of a Newark orphanage, which she had saved from the wreckage of the building. She did not find the stone, but remembered last seeing it used as a bumper for marking parking next to the ark site.

Nearby, at the Evangelical Reform Baptist Church, the preacher welcomed Kea and told the congregation that Kea was "part of the history of this church." People shook her hand admiringly.

I learned from Troy West, a professor of architecture at the New Jersey Institute of Technology, that Murphy Varnish, one of the largest remaining factories in Newark, was being demolished. We visited the nineteenth-century structure, with its red brick exterior and its tall smokestack rising above a field of rubble. Flimsy two-story houses were going up to the north—a vision of the future.

Kea was in an end-of-the-world mood. She advised me to move to the Bronx. How would I get out of Manhattan when the bridges fell and the tunnels were flooded, she asked. Later in the day, I found myself whistling. A music student wanted to know what tune it was. I realized that it was Antonín Dvořák's *New World Symphony*.

284

284 *Kea's Ark, Central Ward of Newark, 1987.*

Selected Bibliography

This is not a full record of the sources I consulted in the course of writing this volume, but will serve as a guide for further reading. Part III deserves mention as a list of works—not necessarily about architecture or the sites I have documented in *American Ruins*—that have a special affinity with my own project. They are provocative works of fiction and nonfiction, and I hope that readers find them as interesting and inspiring as I have.

285 *View along North Gay Street from the roof of the American Brewery, East Baltimore, 1999.*

1. GENERAL SOURCES ON RUINS, ARCHITECTURE,
   AND THE URBAN ENVIRONMENT

Angelini, Bradford L. "Detroit Yesterday and Tomorrow:
    A University of Michigan Planning Exploration."
    Inland Architect, July–August 1991, 38–41.

Banham, Reyner. *A Concrete Atlantis: U.S. Industrial
    Building and European Modern Architecture, 1890–1925.*
    Cambridge, Mass.: MIT Press, 1986.

Baridon, Michel. "Ruins as a Mental Construct." *Journal of
    Garden History,* January–March 1985, 85–96.

Beauregard, Robert A. *Voices of Decline: The Postwar Fate of
    U.S. Cities.* Cambridge, England: Blackwell, 1993.

Bellamy, Edward. *Looking Backward 2000–1887.* New York:
    Penguin Books, 1984.

Belluck, Pam. "Welfare Files Detailing Family Traumas
    Found Discarded." *New York Times,* May 4, 1996.

Benson, Robert. "Mo' Better Town: Detroit in the
    Nineties." *Inland Architect,* July–August 1991, 30–37.

Betzold, Michael. "Soul of the City." *Detroit Sunday
    Journal,* May 17–23, 1998.

Bluestone, Barry, and Bennett Harrison. *The Deindustrial-
    ization of America.* New York: Basic Books, 1982.

Bucci, Federico. *Albert Kahn: Architect of Ford.* New York:
    Princeton Architectural Press, 1993.

Caraley, Demetrios. "Washington Abandons the Cities."
    Political Science Quarterly 107 (spring 1992): 1–30.

Castells, Manuel. "The Informational City Is a Dual City:
    Can It Be Reversed?" In *High Technology and Low-
    Income Communities,* ed. William Mitchell, Donald
    Schön, and Sunyw Bish. Cambridge, Mass.: MIT
    Press, 1999.

Castells, Manuel, and Peter Hall. "Technopoles: Mines
    and Foundries of the Informational Economy." In *The
    City Reader,* ed. Richard T. LeGates and Frederic
    Stout. New York: Routledge, 1996.

Cathcart, James, Frank Fantauzzi, and Terrence Van
    Elslander. "Editing Detroit." *New Observations* 85
    (September–October 1991).

Catlin, Robert. "The Decline and Fall of Gary, Indiana."
    Planning, June 1988, 10–15.

Ciucci, Giorgio, Francesco Dal Co, Mario Manieri-Elia,
    and Manfredo Tafuri. *The American City from the Civil
    War to the New Deal.* Trans. Barbara Luigi La Penta.
    Cambridge, Mass.: MIT Press, 1979.

Claeys, Gregory, ed. *Utopias of the British Enlightenment.*
    Cambridge, England: Cambridge University Press,
    1994.

Desai, Anuj. "Scratch It." *Dodge City Journal* 1, no. 3 (1998):
    52–56.

"Detroit Is Everywhere." Symposium held at the
    Storefront for Art and Architecture, New York, May
    1995.

Dickinson, James. *Journey into Space: Interpretations of
    Landscape in Contemporary Art.* Lawrenceville, N.J.:
    Rider University, 1997.

Dimendberg, Edward. "Kiss the City Goodbye." In *Sites
    & Stations Provisional Utopias: Architecture and Utopia
    in the Contemporary City,* ed. Stan Allen and Kyong
    Park. New York: Lusitania, 1995.

Domosh, Mona. "The Symbolism of the Skyscraper: Case
    Studies of New York's First Tall Buildings." *Journal of
    Urban History* 14, no. 3 (May 1988): 320–45.

Drake, St. Clair, and Horace R. Clayton. *Black Metropolis:
    A Study of Negro Life in a Northern City.* 1945. Reprint,
    New York: Harper Torchbooks, 1962.

Ferriss, Hugh. *The Metropolis of Tomorrow.* New York: Ives
    Washburn, 1929.

Ferry, W. Hawkins. *The Buildings of Detroit: A History.*
    Detroit: Wayne State University Press, 1980.

———. *The Legacy of Albert Kahn.* Detroit: Wayne State
    University Press, 1987.

Fishman, Robert. "Beyond Suburbia: The Rise of the
    Technoburb." In *The City Reader,* ed. Richard T. LeGates
    and Frederic Stout. New York: Routledge, 1996.

———. "Cities after the End of Cities." *Harvard Design
    Magazine,* winter–spring 1997, 14–15.

Frampton, Kenneth. "Intimations of Durability: Notes on
    Architecture and the Theme of Time." *Harvard Design
    Magazine,* fall 1997, 22–28.

Fuerst, J. S., and Roy Petty. "Bleak Housing in Chicago."
    Public Interest 53 (summer 1978): 103–10.

Gropius, Walter. *Apollo in the Democracy: The Cultural
    Obligation of the Architect.* New York: McGraw Hill,
    1968.

Hales, Peter B. "Landscape Documentary: Questions of
    Rephotography." *Afterimage,* summer 1987, 10–3.

Hampson, Rick. "Old Skyscrapers Endangered." *Detroit
    News,* October 24, 1995.

286 *Over-life-size bust of Abraham Lincoln, Englewood, Chicago, 1997. Erected by Phil Blomquist in 1926 on the corner of Wolcott Avenue and Sixty-ninth Street, in front of a Lincoln gas station, the statue has been broken and was even painted black, but was recently painted white again.*

Hanson, David T. *Waste Land: Meditations on a Ravaged Landscape*. New York: Aperture, 1997.

Harbison, Robert. *The Built, the Unbuilt, and the Unbuildable: In Pursuit of Architectural Meaning*. Cambridge, Mass.: MIT Press, 1991.

Harris, Ian, ed. *Edmund Burke: Pre-Revolutionary Writings*. Cambridge, England: Cambridge University Press, 1993.

Heiss, Alanna. *Dennis Oppenheim Selected Works: 1967–1990*. New York: Abrams, 1992.

Hill, Richard Child. "Crisis in the Motor City: The Politics of Economic Development in Detroit." In *Restructuring the City: The Political Economy of Urban Redevelopment*, ed. Susan S. Fainstein and Norman L. Fainstein. White Plains, N.Y.: Longman, 1986.

Hirsch, Arnold R. *Making the Second Ghetto: Race and Housing in Chicago, 1940 to 1960*. Cambridge, England: Cambridge University Press, 1983.

Isaacs, Reginald. *Gropius: An Illustrated Biography of the Creator of the Bauhaus*. Boston: Little, Brown, 1991.

Jackson, J. B. *Landscapes: Selected Writings*. Ed. Ervin H. Zube. Amherst: University of Massachusetts Press, 1970.

———. *The Necessity for Ruins and Other Topics*. Amherst: University of Massachusetts Press, 1980.

Jakle, John A., and Keith A. Sculle. *The Gas Station in America*. Baltimore: Johns Hopkins University Press, 1994.

Kanaley, Reid. "One Meridian Loses Top as Slow Descent Begins." *Philadelphia Inquirer*, July 19, 1998.

King, R. J. "City's Revival May Breathe Life into Detroit's Old Gems." *Detroit News*, May 26, 1998.

Kostof, Spiro. "His Majesty the Pick: The Aesthetics of Demolition." *Design Quarterly* 118–19 (1982): 32–41.

Krieger, Alex. "The American City: Ideal and Mythic Aspects of a Reinvented Urbanism." *Assemblage*, July 1987, 39–58.

LaCloche, Francis. *Architectures de Cinémas*. Paris: Editions du Moniteur, 1981.

Lord, Catherine. "In New Haven, Art Meets Sociology." *Afterimage*, May–June 1998, 6.

Margolies, John. *Pump and Circumstance: Glory Days of the Gas Station*. Boston: Little, Brown, 1993.

Marling, Karal Ann, ed. *Designing Disney's Theme Parks: The Architecture of Reassurance*. New York: Flammarion, 1997.

Mattingly, Katharine Meyer, ed. *Detroit Architecture, AIA Guide*. Detroit: Wayne State University Press, 1971.

Meeks, Carroll L. V. *The Railroad Station: An Architectural History*. New Haven: Yale University Press, 1956.

Meier, Walter R. "Eight Years of Planning for Profit: The Stott Building, Detroit." *American Architect*, September 1930, 44–47, 110.

Mendelsohn, Erich. *Erich Mendelsohn's Amerika*. 1926. Reprint, New York: Dover Publications, 1993.

Montgomery, Lori. "The Beauty of Desolation." *Detroit Free Press,* February 1, 1996.

Mumford, John K. "This Land of Opportunity: Gary, the City that Arose from a Sandy Waste." *Harper's,* July 1908.

Newark Office of Real Property. "Bright Future Property Action, Together We Can Do Anything." Mimeographed article. Newark, 1981.

"New Buildings for 194x." *Architectural Forum,* special issue, May 1943.

Newman, Oscar. *Defensible Space: Crime Prevention through Urban Design.* New York: Collier, 1973.

"Pain and Promises: The Detroit Riot's Legacy." *Detroit Free Press,* July 19, 1987.

Pike, Burton. "The City as Image." In *The City Reader,* ed. Richard T. LeGates and Frederic Stout. New York: Routledge, 1996.

Plunz, Richard A. "Detroit Is Everywhere." *Architecture,* April 1996, 55–61.

Potter, Janet Greenstein. *Great American Railroad Stations.* New York: John Wiley & Sons, 1996.

Public Works Historical Society. *Chicago: An Industrial Guide.* Chicago, 1991.

Roth, Michael S., Claire Lyons, and Charles Merewether. *Irresistible Decay: Ruins Reclaimed.* Los Angeles: Getty Research Institute for the History of Art and the Humanities, 1997.

Schoener, Allen. *Harlem on My Mind.* New York: Random House, 1968.

Schwartzer, Mitchell. "Beyond the Valley of Silicon Architecture." *Harvard Design Magazine,* winter–spring 1999, 15–21.

Seigel, Fred. "A Portrait of Decay." *Weekly Standard,* February 26, 1996.

Sharp, Dennis. *The Picture Palace and Other Buildings for the Movies.* New York: Frederick A. Praeger, 1969.

Simmel, Georg. "The Ruin." In *Georg Simmel, 1858–1918,* ed. Kurt H. Wolff. Columbus: Ohio State University Press, 1959.

Thomson, M. W. *Ruins: Their Preservation and Display.* London: Colonnade, 1981.

VanderBeke, P. K. "Motor City Preservation: Saving Buildings from a Trade-in Mentality." *Inland Architect,* July–August 1991, 42–45.

Walsh, David. "Detroit in Ruins." *International Workers Bulletin,* May 5, 1997, 11.

White, Norval, and Elliot Willensky. *AIA Guide to New York City.* New York: Macmillan, 1978.

Woods, Lebbeus. "Everyday War." In *Mortal City,* ed. Peter Lang. New York: Princeton Architectural Press, 1995.

Yochelson, Bonnie. "What Are the Photographs of Jacob Riis?" *Culturefront* 3 (Fall 1994): 28–36.

287

287 *Vacant building ready for demolition, Henry Horner Homes, Chicago, 1998.*

II. ABOUT THE AMERICAN RUINS PROJECT

Bennet, James. "A Tribute to Ruin Irks in Detroit." *New York Times*, December 10, 1995.

French, Ron. "Artist Sees Downtown as Skyscraper Monument." *Detroit News*, December 12, 1995.

Dickinson, James. "Why Not a Detroit 'Acropolis.'" *New York Times*, December 17, 1995.

"Letters." *Planning*, November 1995, 25.

"Letters." *Planning*, January 1996, 21–23.

Mellish, Xander. "An Artist Tells Detroit Planners: If It's Broke, Please Don't Fix It." *Wall Street Journal*, December 11, 1995.

Vergara, Camilo José. "Tiny Humans, Gigantic Ruins." *Landscape Architecture*, June 1992, 54–55.

———. "Save the Ghost Buildings: Monuments to Defeat or Irreplaceable Bits of the City's Past?" *New York Times*, July 24, 1994.

———. *The New American Ghetto*. New Brunswick, N.J.: Rutgers University Press, 1995.

———. "Downtown Detroit: 'American Acropolis' or Vacant Land—What to Do with the World's Third Largest Concentration of Pre-Depression Skyscrapers?" *Metropolis*, April 1995.

———. "Downtown Detroit: An American Acropolis." *Planning*, August 1995, 18–19.

———. "Tracking New York's Ghettos." In *City Speculations*, ed. Patricia C. Phillips. New York: Princeton Architectural Press, 1996.

———. "Should Detroit Preserve Its Skyscrapers as Ruins?" *Detroit News*, April 13, 1997.

———. "Gorgeous Hulks." *Philadelphia Inquirer*, August 2, 1997.

———. "A Tree Grows in the Heart of Camden Public Library." *Philadelphia Inquirer*, April 18, 1998.

———. "Urbanity in Decay." *Detroit Free Press*, April 28, 1998.

———. "XXth-Century American Ruins." *Harvard Design Magazine*, fall 1997, 63–65.

———. "Studying America in Ruins." *Sacramento Bee Forum*, August 16, 1998.

———. The New American Ghetto Archive at Columbia University. Web site: http://www.columbia.edu/imaging/html/browsers/camilo/camilo-browser.html.

III. INSPIRING WORKS

"The Abandoned County." *Time*, April 29, 1966.

Ballard, J. G. *Crash*. New York: Farrar, Straus and Giroux, 1973.

———. *High Rise*. New York: Carroll & Graf, 1975.

———. *The Terminal Beach*. London: J. M. Dent & Sons, 1984.

Barrientos, Joaquín Alvarez. *Mariano José de Larra Artículos*. Barcelona: Biblioteca Hermes-Clasicos Castellanos, 1997.

Baudelaire, Charles. "Le Cygne." In *Les Fleurs du Mal*. Paris: Editions Rombaldi, 1950.

———. *Petits Poèmes en Prose Oeuvres Critiques Extraits*. Paris: Larousse, 1971.

Benjamin, Walter. "The Work of Art in the Age of Mechanical Reproduction." In *Illuminations*, ed. Hannah Arendt, trans. Harry Zohn. New York: Schocken, 1968.

———. "A Berlin Chronicle," "Paris: Capital of the Nineteenth Century." In *Reflections*, ed. Peter Demetz, trans. Edmund Jephcott. New York: Schocken, 1978.

Benn, Gottfried. "Man and Woman Go through the Cancer Barrack." Trans. Joachim Neugroschel. In *The German Mind of the Nineteenth Century: A Literary and Historical Anthology*, ed. Herman Glaser. New York: Continuum, 1981.

Berman, Marshall. *All that Is Solid Melts into Air: The Experience of Modernity*. New York: Simon and Schuster, 1982.

Borges, Jorge Luis. *Evaristo Carriego*. Buenos Aires: Emecé Editores, 1955.

"Clues: Morelli, Freud, and Sherlock Holmes." In *The Sign of Three: Dupin, Holmes, Pierce*, ed. Umberto Eco and Thomas A. Sebeok. Bloomington: Indiana University Press, 1983.

Douglas, Mary. *Purity and Danger: An Analysis of the Concepts of Pollution and Taboo*. London: Routledge, 1966.

Heine, Heinrich. *Pages Choisies*. Paris: Armand Colin, 1900.

Huysmans, J. K. *A Rebours*. Paris: Garnier-Flammarion, 1978.

Joffe, Josef. "America the Inescapable." *New York Times Magazine*, June 8, 1997.

Kleist, Heinrich von. *The Marquise of O and Other Stories*. Trans. David Luke and Nigel Reeves. Suffolk, England: Penguin Books, 1978.

Manuel, Frank E., and Fritzie P. Manuel. *Utopian Thought in the Western World*. Cambridge, Mass.: Harvard University Press, 1979.

Massachusetts Historical Society. "The Dynamo and the Virgin." In *The Education of Henry Adams*. Boston: Houghton Mifflin, 1918.

Mitchell, Joseph. "The Bottom of the Harbor." In *Up in the Old Hotel and Other Stories*. New York: Vintage, 1993.

Monsivais, Carlos. "Agustin Lara, el Harem Illusorio." In *Amor Perdido*. Mexico City: Biblioteca Era, 1977.

Orwell, George. *Down and Out in Paris and London*. New York: Harcourt Brace, 1933.

288 *Skeletons on Skid Row, Los Angeles, 1997. The mural was painted by the Mojado Brothers after a design by the early-twentieth-century Mexican artist Guadalupe Posada—but with Los Angeles clothes and Los Angeles humor.*

288

Pessoa, Fernando. "The Mariner." Trans. George Ritchie. *Performing Arts Journal* 44 (May 1993): 47–62.

Pierson, George Wilson. "The Exile of Lake Oneida." In *Tocqueville in America*. Baltimore: Johns Hopkins University Press, 1996.

Reyes, Alfonso. "Visión de Anáhuac." In *Antología de Alfonso Reyes*. Mexico City: Fondo de Cultura Económica, 1963.

Riegl, Alois. "The Modern Cult of Monuments: Its Character and Its Origin." *Oppositions* 25 (fall 1982): 20–51.

Riis, Jacob. *How the Other Half Lives*. 1890. Reprint, New York: Dover Publications, 1971.

Rulfo, Juan. *Pedro Paramo*. Mexico City: Fondo de Cultura Economica, 1986.

Ruskin, John. *The Seven Lamps of Architecture*. 1849. Reprint, New York: Farrar, Straus and Giroux, 1984.

Silva, Jose Asuncion. "Nocturno." In *Poemas y Prosas*. Bogotá: Editorial Norma S.A., 1990.

Smithson, Alison and Peter. "But Today We Collect Ads." In *Modern Dreams: The Rise and Fall and Rise of Pop*. Cambridge, Mass.: MIT Press, 1988.

Smithson, Robert. "A Tour of the Monuments of Passaic, New Jersey." In *The Writings of Robert Smithson*, ed. Nancy Holt. New York: New York University Press, 1979.

Taibo, Paco Ignacio, II. *No Habrá Final Feliz*. Mexico City: Editorial Planeta Mexicana, 1995.

Tanizaki, Junichiro. "The Mother of Captain Shigemoto." In *Modern Japanese Literature: From 1868 to the Present Day,* ed. Donald Keene. New York: Grove Press, 1956.

———. *In Praise of Shadows*. Trans. Thomas J. Harper and Edward G. Seidensticker. New Haven: Leete's Island Press, 1977.

Twain, Mark. *The Innocents Abroad or The New Pilgrims' Progress*. New York: Oxford University Press, 1996.

IV. INDIVIDUAL STRUCTURES AND PROJECTS

American Brewery, Baltimore

Bruton, Elsa M. "Weissner (American) Brewery." In *Some Industrial Archeology of the Monumental City & Environs,* ed. Robert M. Vogel. 1975.

Dorsey, John, and James D. Dilts. *A Guide to Baltimore Architecture*. Centreville, Md.: Tidewater Publishers, 1997.

"Gambrinus Still Holds His Tankard in Brewery Niche." *Evening Sun*, August 1, 1929.

"In Heaven They Brew No Beer, Nor Do They Here." *Sunday Sun Magazine*, May 20, 1973.

Pietila, Antero. "And Now?" *The Sun*, July 26, 1975.

Rasmussen, Fred. "Beer Flowed from the 'Storybook Castle.'" *The Sun*, March 15, 1998.

Reutter, Mark. "New Life Planned for Ornate Brewery." *The Sun*, April 29, 1978.

The Western Brewer and Journal of the Barley, Malt, and Hop Trades, May 15, 1887, 10–12.

Art on the Edge: Chicago, Newark, and Detroit

Berman, Marshall. "Views from the Burning Bridge." In *Urban Mythologies: The Bronx Represented since the 1960s*. New York: Bronx Museum of the Arts, forthcoming.

Bronx Borough Courthouse

Dierickx, Mary B. *The Architecture of Public Justice: Historic Courthouses of the City of New York*. New York: City Department of General Services, 1993.

Halbfinger, David M. "Auction Ends 5-Year Dream in 5 Minutes." *New York Times*, March 20, 1998.

Niven, Lisa. "Bronx Borough Courthouse." New York: Landmarks Preservation Commission, 1981.

Brush Park, Detroit

Abraham, Molly. "This Old House Is a Nice New Restaurant." *Detroit Free Press*, December 3, 1992.

Andrews, Sharony. "Historic Mansion Takes a Little Trip." *Detroit Free Press*, March 10, 1993.

Barron, John. "The Evangelist of Alfred Street." *Monthly Detroit*, October 1985.

City of Detroit City Council Historic Designation Advisory Board. Proposed "Brush Park Historic District Final Report," n.d.

Farrell, Michael. "Another Detroit Landmark Doomed." *Spirit*, January 1992.

Hewson, Shirley. "The Art House, Detroit." *Antique Collector*, May 1988.

Kraus, Carolyn. "Patches of Eden amid Detroit's Ruins." *New York Times*, June 25, 1988.

———. "'I See Demolition.'" *Preservation News*, November 1988.

Michigan Department of State, Bureau of History. Information on Domestic/Commercial Architecture, Religious/Social Architecture, Commerce and Economic Affairs and Technology, and Cultural/Humanitarianism and Social Affairs. Information on Alfred Street, Winder Street, Adelaide Street, and Baubien Street.

Michigan Historical Commission. Information on Brush Park history. Miscellaneous archives.

Solokov, Raymond. "Retreading Motown: New Oases in the Urban Desert." *Wall Street Journal*, November 5, 1985.

City Methodist Church, Gary

Lane, James B. *City of the Century: A History of Gary, Indiana.* Bloomington: Indiana University Press, 1978.

Corn Exchange Bank, Harlem

Dolkart, Andrew Scott. *Mount Morris Bank Building.* Ed. Marjorie Pearson. New York: Landmarks Preservation Commission, 1993.

Essex County Jail, Newark

Bennett, Cliff. "Shower Baths Now Stand in Jail's Gallows Corner." *Star-Ledger*, January 8, 1950.

Chamber of Commerce of the United States. *A Handbook on White-Collar Crime: Everyone's Problem, Everyone's Loss.* Washington: Chamber of Commerce of the United States, 1974.

Eldridge, Douglas. "Essex Jail Now Historic Site: Two Methodist Churches Also Selected as Landmarks." *Newark Sunday News*, October 15, 1961.

Herszenhorn, David M. "Confidential Police Records Left Strewn about Ruined Jail." *New York Times*, October 25, 1998.

Firemen's Insurance Headquarters, Newark

Cunningham, John T. *Newark.* Newark: New Jersey Historical Society, 1966.

Milch, Alexander. "Fireman's Fund Leaving Newark Completely." *Sunday Star-Ledger*, April 15, 1973.

Four Vacant Skyscrapers, Detroit

Chesna, James R. "Vacancies Abound at the Book-Cadillac Hotel but No One's Getting In: How I Spent My Summer, Part 2." *Orchard Ridge Recorder*, October 1994.

The Heidelberg Project, Detroit

Beardsley, John. *Gardens of Revelation: Environments by Visionary Artists.* New York: Abbeville, 1995.

Brandow, Michael. "Sweet Charity." *Art News*, May 1992.

Colby, Joy. "High Noon on Heidelberg." *Art and Antiques*, May 1992.

Goldberg, Vicki. "Art by the Block." *Connoisseur*, March 1989.

The Heidelberg Project. Letter to Mayor Dennis Archer, 1998.

The Heidelberg Project. Web site: http://www. heidelberg.org.

Hodges, Michael H. "The Hope of Heidelberg St." *Detroit News*, July 5, 1995.

Sweeny, Ann. "Art Everybody Took Pride In . . . It's Gone." *Detroit News and Free Press*, November 24, 1991.

Templin, Neal. "Are They B. F. Goodrich Retreads or Part of a Genuine Work of Art?" *Wall Street Journal*, November 29, 1991.

Yolles, Sandra. "Junk Magic." *Art News*, October 1989.

J. L. Hudson's Department Store, Detroit

DeHaven, Judy. "Today, We Say Goodbye to Years of Frustration." *Detroit News*, October 25, 1998.

Dixon, Jennifer. "Century-Old Landmark Falls in Seconds." *Detroit Free Press*, October 25, 1998.

Dixon, Jennifer, and Marsha Low. "Rock Solid: For $5, A Piece of Hudson's Can Be Yours." *Detroit Free Press*, October 28, 1998.

Hodges, Michael H. "Hudson's in Its Heyday: Metro Detroiters Cherish Their Memories before Demolition." *Detroit Free Press*, October 22, 1998.

Hyde, Justin. "Hudson's Final Day Will Come in October." *Associated Press*, September 26, 1998.

Montemurri, Patricia. "City Hopes Rubble Makes Way for Rebirth." *Detroit Free Press*, October 26, 1998.

Shepardson, David. "Shoppers Pay Final Respects: Metro Detroiters View Remains of Departed Friend." *Detroit News*, October 26, 1998.

Krueger Brewery, Newark

"Brewery Acquires Belmont School: Lawyer Assigns His Bid on Old Building to Krueger." *Newark News*, June 11, 1946.

Byrd, Frederick W. "Century-Old Brewery Demolished to Clear Space for Shopping Mall." *Star-Ledger*, September 13, 1988.

Longwood, William. "Original Krueger Brewhouse to Become Memory: Site to be Used as Truck Driveway." *Newark News*, April 1, 1949.

"Salute to Krueger: Brewery Observes Century in City." *Newark News*, April 13, 1958.

Walker, Steven T. "Krueger Capsule: 1880 Items Donated to Newark Library." *Star-Ledger*, April 30, 1991.

Krueger Mansion, Newark

Byrd, Frederick W. "Community Groups Still Work to Resurrect Dilapidated Krueger Mansion." *Star-Ledger*, February 4, 1985.

Carter, Barry. "Outlook Brightens for Historic Newark Mansion." *Sunday Star-Ledger*, September 16, 1990.

———. "House on the Hill: Krueger Mansion Restoration Advances with Careful Steps." *Sunday Star-Ledger*, February 13, 1994.

Garrett, Reggie. "A Home for African-American History: 1996 Completion Seen for Krueger-Scott Mansion Renovation; Gathering of Materials Urged." *Star-Ledger*, May 9, 1994.

Krueger Mansion. Web site: http://www.krueger-scott.org.

"Krueger-Scott Mansion: The Jewel of the Central Ward." Rededication ceremony, September 18, 1990.

Patterson, Mary Jo. *Newark's Historical Headache* (four-part series). "Historical Headache: Mansion at Financial Crossroads," "History of the Krueger-Scott Mansion," "Beer Baron Gottfried Krueger," "Entrepreneur Louise Scott." *Star-Ledger*, December 15, 1997.

Sasson, Victor E. "Saving a Landmark from the Ravages of Man." *Bergen Record*, June 15, 1984.

Walker, Steven T. "Barrier-Free Step to History: Radio Station Contributes to Krueger Mansion Renovation." *Star-Ledger*, November 13, 1991.

———. "Krueger Mansion Plan Moving into Phase 2." *Star-Ledger*, May 28, 1995.

Woody, Kenneth. "Newark Council Votes $1 Million for Krueger Mansion Restoration." *Star-Ledger*, June 26, 1985.

Michigan Central Railroad Station, Detroit

Dixon, Jennifer. "Photographer Envisions Old Train Station as Monastery." *Detroit Free Press*, January 20, 1999.

Sachs, Susan. "From Gritty Depot, a Glittery Destination: Refurbished Grand Central Terminal Worthy of Its Name Is Reopened." *New York Times*, October 2, 1998.

Scott, Gerald. "Filmmaker's Next Stop Is Detroit's Old Depot." *Renaissance Times*, April 13, 1998.

Smith, Dena. "A Ticket to the Past: The Old Train Station Reveals Grandeur and Decay at the End of the Line." *Metro Times*, May 15–21, 1996.

Wowk, Mike. "Producers Make Documentary on Former Detroit Train Station." *Detroit News*, May 1, 1998.

Northeastern High School, Detroit

McDonald, Maureen. "City Wise: Detroit's Comeback Bittersweet for Artist Who Specializes in Painting Urban Blight." *Detroit News*, June 5, 1998.

Packard Automobile Plant, Detroit

Gray, Madison J. "Hidden Treasures: Packard Plant Dilemma; A Rebirth or a Razing?" *Detroit News*, September 23, 1998.

Police Youth Bureau, Detroit

Eckert, Katryn Bishop. *Buildings of Michigan*. New York: Oxford University Press, 1993.

RCA Victor's "Nipper" Building, Camden

Kocieniewski, David. "City on Life Support Tries to Rally: Camden, N.J., Seeks to Reverse Four Decades of Decline." *New York Times*, September 15, 1998.

Riviera Theater, Detroit

Stapleford, Richard. *Temples of Illusion: The Atmospheric Theaters of John Eberson; An Exhibition of Original Drawings and Photographs of Silent Movie Theaters*. New York: Bertha and Karl Leubsdorf Art Gallery, Hunter College, April 13–May 27, 1988.

2051 West Lake, Chicago

Andrews, James A. "Agencies with an Attitude." *Planning*, November 1998, 10–14.

Belluck, Pam. "Razing the Slums to Rescue the Residents." *New York Times*, September 6, 1998.

U.S. Department of Housing and Urban Development, Office of Public Affairs. "Henry Extension Buildings Make Way for Redevelopment as Part of HUD's Effort to Revitalize Communities." News release, August 11, 1995.

Vehicles of Desire

Banham, Reyner. "Vehicles of Desire." *Art*, September 1955.

Woodland Cemetery, Newark

Branch, Linda. "Lack of Cash Delays Tombstone Repairs." *Star-Ledger*, May 20, 1990.

Byrd, Frederick. "Welfare Burials Spark Complaints in Central Ward." *Star-Ledger*, October 19, 1971.

Kukla, Barbara. "Cleanup Campaign Begins at Cemetery." *Star-Ledger*, June 17, 1991.

———. "Genealogist Breathes New Life into History of Woodland Cemetery Research: Helps Jerseyan to Set Right Some Myths amid Site Cleanup." *Star-Ledger*, March 6, 1997.

———. "Bringing Woodland Cemetery Back from Dead: Watchdog Group Holds Hope for Rundown Facility." *Star-Ledger*, November 20, 1997.

Walker, Steven T. "Neglected Cemetery: Newark Man Points out Woodland Woes." *Sunday Star-Ledger*, June 9, 1991.

"Your Mother!"

Freifeld, Karen. "As Subtle as a Slap in the Face." *New York Newsday*, May 21, 1995, city edition.

Acknowledgments

American Ruins was a precarious undertaking from the start, and many helped me, including those who had only the vaguest idea of what I was doing. Foremost was Charles Pieroni (who first regarded my interest as a hobby and later, as it persisted, as a reflection of my peculiar character), who generously pitched in with financial help. A remarkable self-made lawyer and businessman, Charlie slept many times at Detroit's Statler Hilton and Book-Cadillac Hotels and frequented the area's famous steak houses and restaurants. As I return to those buildings, I can hear him telling me, "That was a nice place; that was a real nice place. I wonder what happened to it?" And I imagine his mind teeming with memories of tall buildings, busy streets, and elegant stores.

Others know the structures and the landscapes I have documented and are moved by the neglect, the bulldozing, and the implosions that alter them. Kea Tawana, who miraculously reappeared in my life after an absence of ten years, was just what I needed to finish this book. Tim Samuelson, curator of architecture at the Chicago Historical Society, shared his accounts not only of the midwestern buildings and landscapes he knows so well but also of the people and the trades behind the decline. Tim's examples gave color and concreteness to my abstractions. He also lent me the key to his Chicago apartment and told me to "just show up."

In downtown Detroit Matt Pieroni and Virginia Auvil-Pieroni told me repeatedly, "You know you are always welcome here." And Tony Pieroni always welcomed me to Detroit and sent me a steady flow of articles about the city. Gina and Gemma Pieroni put me up at their house in Oak Park, Illinois, every year, for weeks at a time, for two decades running.

My gratitude extends to those who accompanied me on tours of abandoned buildings, making it much easier to experience the places and photograph the structures. Special thanks are due to Harold Bauder of Wayne State University. The late John Everett, head of security at Harbor Light, a drug-treatment facility in Detroit's Cass Corridor, let me go to the roof to take a series of skyline views.

I also thank those who regularly send me newspaper clippings, notify me of impending implosions, and give me personal accounts of what they have seen. Principal among these is James Dickinson, professor at Rider University, who over the past five years has kept me informed about Philadelphia's relentless decay and has sent me reviews of art shows and books on such diverse topics as entropy, ruination, and the sublime.

Year after year friends have written letters of recommendation for grants. Columbia University professor Kenneth T. Jackson has also toured Newark, New York City, and Los Angeles with me; professor Robert Fishman of Rutgers read drafts of my book, advised me on how to improve it, suggested places I should go, and even came with me to some of the ruins; and Daniel Bluestone's inspired lectures on the history of American architecture at Columbia were both a pleasure and a challenge.

I could not have completed this book without the help and generosity of many institutions. The Graham Foundation's grants came at crucial times. Its longtime director Carter H. Manny was always supportive and kind. The Richard H. Driehaus Foundation, through its director, Sunny Fischer, also contributed greatly to making this book possible. Sunny arranged for the Joyce and Fannie Mae Foundations to fund the purchase of a selection of my Chicago photographs by the Chicago Historical Society.

Others saw me grapple with ideas and helped to clarify them. Foremost among these is Lisa Vergara, an art historian who patiently read through my prose and curbed some of my more moralistic impulses. Often she could not see in my images what I saw in them, which sometimes led me to rephotograph or replace them. Dennis Nawrocki invited me to participate in a show on Detroit at the Gallery at the Center for Creative Studies in Detroit in 1997. Dennis knows many of the places I describe, and his comments on an early version of my text were invaluable.

In 1998, Joan Ockman, director of Columbia's Buell Center for the Study of American Architecture, invited me to do an exhibition on downtown Detroit entitled "Urbanity in Decay." The gallery talk I gave at her invitation provided me with an opportunity to discuss my work with the students and faculty of the Columbia University Graduate Program of Historic Preservation. At Columbia, I also met preservationist Garrick Landsberg, who became my friend and companion in visits to abandoned buildings in Detroit and Newark.

Others who helped me identify meanings in the forest of images and interviews I collected were professors Marshall Berman of the City University of New York, Charles Hoch of the University of Illinois, Chicago, Gary Sands of Wayne State University in Detroit, Howard Gillette of Rutgers University, William Saunders of Harvard University, and James Lane of Indiana University Northwest. Rebecca Binno, a Detroit preservationist, generously shared with me her vast knowledge of Detroit buildings. Julie Lasky read several sections and offered many valuable suggestions, and Esha Janssens faithfully helped during the last stages of manuscript preparation; with her assistance it became a more ambitious book. I would also like to thank my editors at The Monacelli Press, Miranda Robbins and Andrea Monfried.

Preliminary essays were given a home at the *Sacramento Bee*, *Print Magazine*, the *Michigan Quarterly Review*, *City Limits*, the *Harvard Design Magazine*, *Architectural Record,* and the opinion pages of the *Philadelphia Inquirer* and the *Detroit Free Press*.

While working on this book many generous people provided insight into the buildings and their contexts that added richness to my experiences. I have tried to avoid making inferences without first checking with those who seem to know more. *American Ruins* reflects differences of opinion and interpretation; I never shied away from giving my own views and impressions.